T0165988

THE FORGOTTEN GENERATION

From South Vietnamese to Vietnamese-American

Vui Le

iUniverse, Inc.
New York Bloomington

The Forgotten Generation
From South Vietnamese to Vietnamese-American

Copyright © 2009 Vui Le

All rights reserved. No part of this book may be used or reproduced by any means, graphic, electronic, or mechanical, including photocopying, recording, taping or by any information storage retrieval system without the written permission of the publisher except in the case of brief quotations embodied in critical articles and reviews.

Publisher's Note

This book is designed to provide information about the subject matter covered. It is sold with the understanding that the publisher and author are not engaged in rendering psychological, financial, legal, or other professional services. If expert assistance is needed, the services of a competent professional should be sought.

iUniverse books may be ordered through booksellers or by contacting:

iUniverse
1663 Liberty Drive
Bloomington, IN 47403
www.iuniverse.com
1-800-Authors (1-800-288-4677)

Because of the dynamic nature of the Internet, any Web addresses or links contained in this book may have changed since publication and may no longer be valid. The views expressed in this work are solely those of the author and do not necessarily reflect the views of the publisher, and the publisher hereby disclaims any responsibility for them.

ISBN: 978-1-4401-6860-4 (pbk)
ISBN: 978-1-4401-6859-8 (cloth)
ISBN: 978-1-4401-6861-1 (ebook)

Printed in the United States of America
iUniverse rev. date: 8/27/09

For my wife and family

Qua Đèo Ngang

Bước tới Đèo Ngang, bóng xế tà,
Cỏ cây chen đá, lá chen hoa.
Lom khom dưới núi, tiều vài chú,
Lác đác bên sông, rợ mấy nhà.
Nhớ nước đau lòng, con quốc quốc,
Thương nhà mỏi miệng, cái gia gia.
Dừng chân đứng lại, trời, non, nước,
Một mảnh tình riêng, ta với ta.

-- Bà Huyện Thanh Quan

Crossing Ngang Pass

Arriving at Ngang Pass before dark
Among the rocks, bushes and flowers
Several monks working at the foot of the hill
Few huts dotting the landscape across the river
My heart aches for my country
My soul longs for my home
Stopping here in this heavenly country
A sentiment of mine and me

(Loosely translated)

Prologue

I learned this Vietnamese poem, *Qua Đèo Ngang*, during the years of my studies at An Phong Học Viện, a Catholic Redemptorist Seminary just outside of my home city of Saigon. I was twelve or thirteen then so I cannot quite remember all of the words, but I certainly remember the sentiment.

My heart aches for my country ...

The poem describes a traveler's feelings when she passes through a rural area that reminds her of her home country.

My soul longs for my home ...

In a sense, we are all travelers, refugees or expatriates. We are either going somewhere, running from something, or leaving things behind at sometime or another during our lifetime. It would be so nice to take a rest once in a while to appreciate what we have, wherever we are, and perhaps even to reminisce.

This book is dedicated to the forgotten generation of Vietnamese Expatriates who fought valiantly for South Vietnam, risked their lives in search of freedom, and made sacrifices for the future of their children.

May God look kindly upon you and give you Peace.

Les Gabriels, this photograph was taken in 1972
at An Phong Học Viện,
Thủ Đức, Việt Nam

*The author is standing on the last row second to the right.
Reverend Director of the Juvenate Peter Đặng Văn Đào is on the
far left and Father Yuse Nguyễn Tiến Lộc is on the far right.*

CHAPTER ONE

Preparation

One day in late March of 1975, my Mom called Cha Đào (Monsignor Dao) and asked him to release me from An Phong Học Viện, a seminary in Thủ Đức, a small city several miles outside of Saigon, where I was a seminarian studying to become a Catholic Priest. The old priest, a relative who ran the seminary, called me to his office and, without explanation, said:

"Con về đi, Má cần con ở nhà." Go home. Your mother needs you.

Confused and perplexed, I left my seminarian friends behind and took the bus home. All the while, I was scared as my Mom had never done this to me before. I was an excellent student and getting along reasonably well with everyone. The priests had always complained about my being too assertive, but Mom knew all about those complaints. For years, Mom and Dad paid my tuition in one lump sum at the beginning of each year; and for that, the priests had had a hard time letting me go, as they could not afford to make a refund.

The school year of 1974-1975 was particularly hard on the priests and teachers at An-Phong. Donations from support groups and from the Vietnamese Catholic Church dried up quickly, as everyone and every institution in Vietnam was anticipating the advance of the North Vietnamese Communist forces. It was difficult for the priests to keep us focused on our religious training and shield us from current events. Incidents of civil unrest had become regular occurrences in

1

Saigon. Every month, there were multiple *biểu tình* student protests and *tự thiêu* self incinerating suicides by Buddhist monks.

Once during a trip back to Saigon to visit the family, I came to an intersection where a massive commotion was taking place. People everywhere were pouring out into the street, running, yelling and waving their hands calling on other people to join them. They were excited and scared amid the confusion. Women and men dropped whatever they were doing and rushed out to to get a better look.

"Về kêu bà con lẹ lên, chớ không hết chỗ bây giờ!" someone nearby yelled out. Hurry up. Go get your folks before it's too late!

Curious, I joined the crowd and asked an old man next to me, *"Có chuyện gì vậy Chú?"* What is going on?

He paused and gave me a puzzled look as if I was supposed to know what was going on, and then he pushed his way into the crowd without answering.

A truck full of yellow-robed monks pulled up and stopped right at the center of the intersection. About thirty monks jumped out quickly one after another and formed a large circle at the center of the four-way crossroads.

People all around became talkative and excited as though they knew something of significance was about to happen. People in cars, trucks, on mopeds, bicycles and pedestrians came to a complete stop. Old men, ladies, business people and children formed circles behind the monks, but there was no police officer that I could see. I climbed on top of a metal newspaper stand and held onto the light pole at the corner of the intersection to get a better look.

As the truck drove away, I saw an elderly monk dressed in a traditional Buddhist yellow robe sitting solemnly in the center of the traffic circle. On each side of him a somber, younger monk wearing a similar garment sat on the hot asphalt. The older monk began to chant Buddhist prayers, and soon all the monks were chanting loudly.

"Nam Mô A Di Đà Phật, Nam Mô A Di Đà Phật ..." Praise to Budhist, they sang, and before long, older people in the crowd sat down and joined in.

A couple of minutes passed, and the two younger monks at the center stood up and pulled out small canisters of gasoline from under their robes. The crowd went wild. Some people started to cry, while others gasped loudly in shock. Women frantically covered their children's eyes while others rushed the smaller kids out of view.

A man standing next to me told me to get off the newspaper stand, and I politely refused.

The two monks poured the gasoline on the elder monk as he sat there chanting calmly. The gasoline soaked his robe and changed its color to a darkened orange, almost red as it clung to the monk's body. The smell of gas penetrated the air, and the monks sitting on the perimeter droned louder and louder.

"Nam Mô A Di Đà Phật, Nam Mô A Di Đà Phật, Nam Mô A Di Đà Phật, Nam Mô A Di Đà Phật, Nam Mô A Di Đà Phật, Nam Mô A Di Đà Phật ..." they cried, and the crowd added their voices to the uproar.

Peacefully, the elder monk reached under his robe and took out a lighter. His eyes remained closed and his chanting continued rhythmically. The other monks were now jabbering deafeningly while still sitting. The noise from the crowd grew louder as men and women cried out uncontrollably. Some wept openly; others covered their mouths in horror. It seemed as though the whole earth shook and wept for what was about to happen.

With a gentle flick of the lighter, the flames exploded in all directions around the old monk. He sat there in the middle of the fireball and the vision of his burning body was instantly seared into the memories of hundreds of Vietnamese who stood dumbfounded. Yet the old monk did not move. He did not cry out. The old monk was simply burned to death of his own will.

Black smoke billowed into the clear sky, as the awful acrid smell of burning flesh permeated the area. Men, women and children wept and comforted each other. The earlier astonishment on their faces had yielded to a look of sad resignation. Older men stood up and bowed deeply toward the center of the intersection where the old monk's remains were shrinking.

Now they prayed softly, *"Nam Mô A Di Đà Phật, Nam Mô A Di Đà Phật ..."*

We could hear the sirens of police and fire engines wailing loudly in the distance, as if to mourn the death of an old monk. In a hurried manner, the other monks gathered around the charred body and delicately wrapped him in a linen cloth. The truck they came in backed up slowly and the monks carefully loaded the body onto it. Then, as earlier, the monks one by one formed a single line and in an orderly fashion re-boarded the truck and drove away.

There were no religious or political speeches, no banners, no loud announcements, just flabbergasted onlookers standing around aimlessly, unable to comprehend what their eyes had just witnessed.

When the police finally arrived, the crowd dispersed and the intersection was inundated with normal heavy traffic as if nothing unusual had happened.

I jumped down from the newspaper stand, still dazed from what I had seen. As an eighth grade student, I was not equipped to understand the reasoning and implications of such an event, but I was thoroughly shaken by it. In my mind, I could not understand why no one had stopped the suicide of a gentle monk.

In a country where more than 80 percent of the population was non-Christian, I felt lonelier than ever being a Catholic and not quite comprehending the meaning of sacrifice by suicide. I was taught that it was a sin, but in observing the reverence of the people toward the elderly monk, I could not help but admire his profound courage and his remarkable willingness to die for his cause.

Then I thought about my Dad and his willingness to sacrifice for our country. A tremendous sadness overtook me, and I turned and walked away, wiping tears from my eyes.

The year 1975 was a difficult year for all Vietnamese. The Communist North Vietnamese had stepped up its attacks in the South, and more often each day, the sounds of gunfire could be heard closer to the cities. People of all ages were frightened by the news while convoys of soldiers and artilleries could be seen crisscrossing the countryside.

Everyday, dozens of American GMC trucks filled with Vietnamese soldiers rumbled down Highway 1 on the outskirts of town. They were escorted by heavy M1 and T-41 tanks and personnel carriers that shook the earth as they drove by. Unlike times before, the army rangers did not smile and wave to the people; instead they sat quietly with apprehensive looks on their faces.

In the city, the air was thick with anxiousness. Many businesses and shops had closed, their metal folding doors shut tightly behind the hastily hand-written signs that read:

— *Đóng Cửa, Xin Trở Lại Ngày Khác*

— Closed, Please Come Back Another Day

The open market was more crowded than ever, as people bargained and stocked up on supplies. Churches and temples were full of people at all times of the day. Children were running around, as their parents had taken them out of school and made them stay close. Old men gathered at sidewalk cafés to listen to the news and gossip. And the lines at the banks spilled out into the streets. At Tân Sơn Nhất International Airport and Bến Bạch Đằng (Saigon Seaport), thousands of people stood in line for hours waiting to leave the country.

At my old school An Phong, the priests and other teachers had instructed us to pray, make sacrifices and ask God for help. Everyday, while we calmly prayed for our nation and its people, I could not help but notice the troubled looks on the faces of these peaceful teachers.

All year long I had been a good student, a team leader for my class; I studied hard and ranked first in my class in many subjects. From the early morning's math and science classes to the afternoon's Vietnamese Language, History and Music Appreciation classes to my dreaded Conversational French lectures taught by my favorite, Father Tiến Lộc, I had done well. Even Father Tiến Lộc, a young talented priest who could speak several languages, was pleasantly surprised by my dedication to his subject that year.

The only subject in which I did not excel in was Theology; however, no grade was given in that subject. To many of my classmates, Theology class was the most important one. The priests used these lectures to select the seminarians whom they would invite back the following year. I was just not one of them.

It was only a couple more weeks until the end of the school year, and I knew for certain that I would receive many academic honors. At the beginning of the year, I'd made a promise to make my parents proud; so when Father Đào called me to his office and let me go, I knew it must be something of great importance for Mom to take me out of school at such time.

I asked the bus driver to drop me off at Thị Nghè near Sở Thú (Vietnam National Zoo) and started to wander the streets of Saigon making my way back to our home near Chợ Lớn. I saw soldiers, policemen, public workers and civilians constructing concrete barricades throughout town. Wherever no concrete barriers were available, people built makeshift blockades out of wood and barbed wire. These structures were designed to stop trucks and tanks from entering the city, but, at the same time, they caused widespread havoc and massive traffic jams for citi residents.

Meanwhile people were nailing their windows shut with wooden boards. Some went as far as using barbed wire along their fences. Walking through Saigon that late March, among the heavy traffic noises, I could hear the clatter of hammers pounding and of construction equipment thundering. It was an unnatural symphony from a city desperate to do something to protect itself.

Yet Saigon was still beautiful. I remember rows and rows of tall tamarind trees with red-striped yellow flowers lining streets, throwing soft shade onto the ground leading to majestic buildings and parks. In the courtyards of people's houses, tall plumeria plants had started to yield their first yellow and deeply pink flowers and filled the air with a sweet gentle fragrance.

I walked past the US Embassy, a huge building with high walls. Two American marines with semi-automatic M16s assault riffles stood guard on each side of the main gate. Millions of families both in the North and in the South would be affected by the decisions made behind these walls and perhaps in buildings like these in a land so far away. Down the street stood Dinh Độc Lập Independence Hall, where the president of South Vietnam and his family resided. It was a beautiful building built in a traditional French colonial low-rise style with elaborate decorative windows and expansive front steps. This was another place where decisions were being made that would affect millions of Vietnamese. I thought of my Dad and all that he was fighting for and silently said a prayer for him, wherever he was.

I took a left turn and stopped by Nhà Thờ Đức Bà (Vietnamese National Cathedral). It was a graceful looking church in the center of Saigon. The French built it with the dramatic trappings of Notre Dame in Paris. In front, there was a park and at the center of the park, an enormous statue of Mary standing on a huge red marble pedestal holding the earth in her hands, looking up to heaven as if she were handing it to God. The inside of the Church was dark, serene and peaceful.

My Mom had taken the older kids including me to attend mass here on many occasions. It was where the rich and powerful Vietnamese Catholics in Saigon went to see and be seen. Every Sunday, people dressed up in their best Sunday's clothes with men in western suits and women in their best traditional Áo-Dài (national Vietnamese dresses that are long flowing down to the ankles and have splits on both sides going back to the waists, usually worn with either white or black satin pants). The famous and the wannabes came early to make sure that other people could see them sitting up in the front rows.

Vietnam National Cathedral
Nhà Thờ Đức Bà

The masses were often long and boring, but everyone sat attentively. After mass, my Mom always called a taxi and took us to Chợ Bến Thành (Ben Thanh Market) nearby. Of course, we could have walked the six or seven blocks to it, but my Mom made sure that other people saw we were taxiing away in our best clothes.

I followed the familiar paths and made my way to Chợ Bến Thành. Saigon's central market was a large non-air-conditioned structure that covered three square city blocks. The French built the market for people to congregate and buy and sell their goods. Over the years, it accumulated permanent kiosks with rows of fresh meats and fish next to rows of fruits, vegetables and flowers.

Exotic tropical fruits filled the air with an odd mixture of fragrant and pungent odors. During the early spring, the foul smell of durian could be both inviting to some, yet offensive to others. Strangely enough, it tasted good. Then there were areas for baked goods and pastries. The fresh smells of French bread and pastries were alluring. Vendors and shoppers bargained in good spirit, as though the act of purchasing was a team sport. People laughed out loud as vendors gathered their purchases and packaged them. In the far corner, there were souvenir kiosks selling artwork and gadgets. Then there were vendors selling handmade toys from China. There were even kiosks for clothing and shoes. Throughout Chợ Bến Thành there was an orderly chaos, as people wandered back and forth by the hundreds, yet it was very authentic Vietnamese.

Chợ Bến Thành

On those Sundays, my Mom took us there to eat bánh cuốn (a thin rice cake dish) and to shop. She used to bargain with the vendors and made jokes with the owners who knew her. Her first phrase was always:

"Sao mắc quá vậy cô?" Why so expensive?

To which a vendor would answer, *"Rẻ mà Người Đẹp. Cô Sáu mua một, tôi tặng một nhé."* It's nothing, Pretty One. Cô Sáu, buy one get one free, okay?

The vendors knew my Mom by Cô Sáu, which was her ranking order in her family. In our Vietnamese tradition, the first name of the person is often reserved for close members or friends of the family only. Then my Mom would say, *"Cô Hai lúc nào cũng mua một tính hai phải không?"* You always sell one, but ring up two, Cô Hai?

The word *"hai"* means "two" in Vietnamese. Then they both laughed as my Mom gave the vendor the money in exchange for the merchandise. And just like that, my Mom shopped and had fun with the vendors of Chợ Bến Thành.

There was a gigantic roundabout in front of Chợ Bến Thành, where people on bicycles, mopeds, and in taxis, cars and trucks of all types and sizes competed for every inch of concrete. It was the main intersection in town where more than a half dozen major streets came together. Big trucks inched forward slowly, as mopeds weaved in and out, bumping and pushing into each other. Sometimes traffic came to a standstill when people rushed to cross the massive roundabout. I would not dare. I made my way farther along the streets to find a slow intersection to cross over.

Our home was on a major street called Trần Hưng Đạo. This is the main boulevard connecting Saigon and Chợ Lớn. Along the streets were numerous movie theaters and rạp-hát cải-lương (live theater houses) with colorful signage and there were people coming and going in all directions.

I enjoyed the traffic, the noise and the street vendors. Little did I know that it was my last goodbye to the town that I loved.

When I arrived home, my beautiful mother told me the reason she had wanted me home: since the Communists overran the northern town of Quảng Trị where my Dad was stationed, she had not heard from my father for more than a month. She said we needed to start planning my Dad's funeral.

Heartbroken, Mom's voice cracked with pain, but her composure remained cool, calm and dignified. She looked far away, as if to call on my Dad. Her tears silently trickled down her face, but her commands were courtly delivered. She tried hard not to fall apart in front of her kids, yet I knew she must be in great distress. For years, she had raised the eight of us by herself, as my Dad was rarely home due to his duties as an army officer. She was both a father and a mother to us, and this time she might have to plan for our survival without our Dad.

My Mom was a sophisticated and wealthy lady. She grew up in a family of six children in Nha Trang, a spectacular resort town by the ocean in the middle of the country. Nha Trang has miles of crystal white sandy beach looking out to the deep blue waters of the Pacific Ocean. Several miles from the bay, there are a series of small islands where people fish and enjoy the privacy of stretches of unspoiled beaches. The people of Nha Trang enjoyed the convenience of a large city but maintained the hospitality of a small town. My Mom's side of the family had lived there for generations.

My Mom Nguyễn Thị Khánh in 1954

My maternal Grandfather Ông Ngoại was an old Catholic autocrat full of traditions and discipline. My Grandmother died when Mom was only three-years-old, so Grandfather raised my Mom and her siblings by himself the best way he knew how: with the vigorous and strict rules of a traditional, wealthy and educated Vietnamese family.

Rules like: we had to sit up straight at the dining table and wait until he picked up the chopsticks first before we could pick up ours. There was no loud talking at the table and absolutely no running inside the house. We had to bow our heads everytime we saw or greeted him. Before we went out, we had to go to him, bow our heads and ask for permission. Likewise, we had to do the same whenever we got back. Our Mom would hear about it if we missed or messed up the proper protocols. Strangely enough, we missed these rules after we moved south to the busy city of Saigon.

My Mom used to take us to visit Ông Ngoại every summer at his venerable stately home. He was happy to receive us but also aloof and formal in the way he conducted himself. There were never hugs or kisses, just polite recognition and nods, and sometimes a pat on the head. My Mom loved him dearly and always brought him fancy gifts of fine china or expensive imported teas.

Our visits often caused a big commotion in that little community. When our Citroën DS car turned the corner down the road to Ông Ngoại's home, the children who lived near the main road raced after us. Then nearby neighbors came by to say hello and brought more people with them. Soon word got out that Cô Sáu (my Mom) was home, and curious onlookers stopped by and watched. They stood in the front courtyard and behind the fence for hours gawking at us. Some shambled in to greet my Mom and Dad; others shook hands with my Dad and asked about current events.

On these occasions, Ông Ngoại would tell us kids to ignore them; meanwhile he greeted them with broad smiles, holding his head a little higher. These trips always brought Ông Ngoại pride and my Mom joy. My Dad loved to take us there every summer.

Like my Mom, Dad also came from a wealthy and powerful family in Nha Trang. Our paternal Grandfather Ông Nội died at an early age, and my Dad was brought up by his older brothers Bác Ba and Bác Bốn. Bác Ba was a wealthy farmer who owned land and farms throughout Central Vietnam, while Bác Bốn was a powerful parish priest. They were a family of farmers, priest and patriots. My Dad was a career military man. He graduated valedictorian of his Officer Class at Đà Lạt National Military Academy and served in the South Vietnamese Armed Forces for 25 years. During his service, he was a mayor of several important provinces throughout South Vietnam. He also commanded regiments of Marines and Ranger Forces at the front line.

My Dad Thiếu-Úy Lê Công Chính in 1955

My Mom and Dad met through an ancient, traditional prearranged marriage designed for two families of equal social status. My Dad was a young officer with high ambition and my Mom was a beautiful girl well-trained in household management. My Dad first saw Mom at church on Sundays and tried to strike up a conversation after mass, but a proper young lady did not dare hang out after church to talk to boys. So my Dad wrote Ông Ngoại and asked permission to talk to her.

When my Dad found out that she was available, he asked the village priest to make arrangements for the engagement ceremony and a year later they were married. They fell madly in love and had eight children: four boys and four girls. I am the fourth child of the family.

My Dad and his first four kids in Long Thành

My older brother Hưng and I were born in Nha Trang before my Dad moved the family to the South. In 1962, he was the mayor of Long Thành, a prosperous district south of Saigon. My sister Huyền, who eventually became an Optometrist, was born in this district, and she was the first of four more southern-born children.

One day on the way back to Long Thành from Saigon, my Dad came upon a car that was flipped over in a ditch by the roadside. The driver had suffered massive injuries and was in desperate need of immediate medical care. My Dad and his bodyguard loaded the man into their Jeep and rushed him to the hospital in Long Thành. The man turned out to be of French nationality and the owner of several large rubber tree plantations near Long Thành.

Upon his recovery, he found my Dad to thank him for saving his life. As a gesture of gratitude, he deeded to my Dad several of his plantations. The income generated by these plantations boosted my family's standard of living and gave us a tremendous head start in the South. The Frenchman went back to France and we never heard from him again.

Meanwhile my Dad continued to serve in the Armed Forces and governed several other major districts in South Vietnam. My Mom invested wisely in real estate and commerce. Soon, she bought several residences in Saigon, one of which was a four storied high-rise on one of the busiest main streets in Saigon for our primary residence. On the first level, she operated a wildly successful beauty parlor, and we lived upstairs. Her business initially was a hobby to serve her wealthy friends in a booming Saigon; then it turned into a cash cow as movie stars and other celebrities frequented her shop. Soon the business consumed all of her time and made her even more famous in the circle of Saigon elite.

By the early 1960s, my Dad's service required him to be away from home for months at a time. And with six little children who were always bickering, it was difficult for my Mom. Mom decided to put the four older kids in Catholic boarding school so the nuns could take care of us. She hired nannies to look after my two younger sisters Huyền and Huyên (Tí), who were not yet in school and lived at home.

The nuns were mean and strict at Thánh Linh Private Catholic School. When someone talked in class when he shouldn't have, he got whacked with a squared ruler as discipline. If you dozed off during prayer time, the nuns pinched your ears. At night, they glided silently back and forth in the sleeping hall trying to catch anyone who would not sleep or lay still. I was only five-years-old and developed a really bad attitude. I cried all the time and refused to do anything the nuns asked me to do. Their punishments did not frighten me, so the nuns often made me sit facing the corner of the classroom.

It was disheartening to look out the classroom windows at my house and see my little sisters, who were not much younger, playing on the terrace, but yet I could not go home. And the nuns could not understand why I was sad or troublesome all the time. Luckily, my family was wealthy, so the nuns could not kick me out of school. Instead, as a punishment they made me repeat kindergarten. That got me in serious trouble with my Mom. She thought I was slow or crazy or both.

My older sister Lêvi was about the only person that really took care of me during that time. A couple of years ago, at the Confirmation of Andrea, Lêvi's only daughter, I wrote the following piece to honor my sister for all she had done for me:

> *Dear Andrea:*
>
> *God loves you so much that He has made you the special one daughter for my sister Lêvi. Although it might feel otherwise to you at times, believe me, you are blessed to be with such wonderful person. Let me tell you why.*
>
> *I was a middle kid in a large family. Remember how sometimes you feel suffocated by all the attention and demand placed upon you as the only child. I was longing for such attention growing up. I was placed in a boarding school since I started kindergarten. Bà Nội was so busy that Chị Vy (your Mom) was the only mother that I knew.*
>
> *While I was a big kid, I got sick easily. Have you ever gotten sick and the world seemed to have abandoned you? That feeling multiplies when you are in a boarding school without your parents. Chị Vy was there to help me with my bedwetting problem, my rough playing, my angry and aggressive manner, my bullying ways and especially my homesickness. Many times your Mom was called away from her classes to wash my soiled clothing, to answer to the*

nuns for my bad behavior, and to comfort me when I just cried and refused to do anything. And she was only ten-years-old.

Then I was off to the seminary. Ask your Mom how often she had taken me to the bus depot and gave me money to spend. Ask her how often she had patted me on the head and tried to hide her tears when I kept asking her why our Mom never comes to visit.

When we first got to America, Chị Vy worked at a Chinese restaurant, and even today, every time I go out to eat at a restaurant, I cannot help but think about the hard work your Mom had endured to help our family. She studied hard as well. I was so proud the day your Mom got accepted to Dental School, and later became a Dentist. Ask her how she had done this while working more than full time and helping out the family.

During this time, she was more than an inspiration for me; she was also my confidant. She encouraged me to be independent and taught me to be courageous in accepting responsibilities. I went to college at Texas A&M against my Mother's wishes, but knew that I was doing the right thing for me. When I met Cô Dung (my wife) in college, it was your Mom that told me to follow my heart.

I love your Mom dearly, because she was also more than an older sister. She was my best Mom. And this is why you are so lucky to have her as a Mom.

Andrea, as you are about to receive Confirmation, thank God for all that He has given you. In confirming your faith in God, hold on to your Mom and confirm your love for her. Do so, not just for yourself, but also for me.

Cậu Vui

My sister Lêvi has a warm spot in my heart. Ever since I was a little kid in Vietnam, I adored her. Her caring personality and her passion to help others made her my role model. She is so much like my Dad: a gentle and loving soul.

When my Mom told me that she had not heard from my Dad for more than a month, I was devastated. I was also angry at the Communists for causing such personal loss, as well as all the other pain and suffering to the people of South Vietnam. The War was meaningless to me, but the misery of my family was very real. I missed my Dad so much and I cried.

The War was nearing its end, and the Communists were winning on the battle fronts, as well as in the hearts and minds of some factions of the population. The government of South Vietnam had become so corrupt that some of its citizens had lost faith in its ability to govern and provide protection for the people. It seemed as though every week another monk had killed himself. Students from various universities protested and paraded in parts of the town. Everyday these protests grew larger and became more violent. The students clashed with the police, interrupted traffic and disrupted business. All the while, they carried banners demanding peace. I had a strong sense that the Communists had infiltrated and encouraged the students' protests. Out in the countryside, the battles between the South Vietnamese Army and Việt Cộng (VC) also became more bloody and decisive, with the VC winning more ground and becoming more emboldened.

In 1973 and 1974, my Dad had volunteered to go to the front line to command several regiments of Marines and Special Forces in Kontum and Pleiku. Later he was stationed in Đà Nẵng (Danang), a large northern city near the demilitarized zone (DMZ). There was a huge American base there, and that made me feel fairly confident that my Dad was safe. But in early 1975, as the war escalated, my Dad again volunteered to go even closer to the battleground. He mobilized his soldiers to Quảng Trị, just miles south of the DMZ.

The Communist North Vietnamese overran the DMZ in February of 1975 and started moving south. In no time at all, they overwhelmed

Quảng Trị, and within days, they overtook Danang as well. With the momentum of these victories, they fearlessly advanced southward through Central Vietnam and then farther south toward Saigon.

The news caused panic in Saigon, and my Mom cried for days worrying about my Dad and our relatives in Nha Trang. She dreaded dealing with our family's real estate holdings throughout the country, as there was not much she could do to save them. Banks were closing everywhere and people stood in line for days trying to withdraw cash and make transfers. She had so much responsibility. Her children were many and small. My youngest sister Hà was just nine-months-old and my little brother Huy Hoàng was only two.

My Mom in 1970

My Mom let her servants and beauty shop workers go home to their families to prepare for what was to come. There was no one to cook, shop and take care of us kids except for Mom. Meanwhile our relatives from Nha Trang took refuge at our residence. My Mom's older brother Cậu Năm, his wife and ten children, and my Mom's younger sister Dì Bảy, her husband and her eight children, all came to stay with us. She missed my Dad and just could not handle such a large gathering. At the same time, she was at a loss for how we were going to survive after the Communist takeover. Nothing used to bother my Mom, but now she locked herself in her bedroom and cried for hours.

It was late in the afternoon one day in April, and we were all gathered around upstairs in our family room. The kids were bored and the adults were scared and didn't know what to do. According to the TV news, the Communists and the South Vietnamese forces were locked in a fierce battle at Xuân Lộc only miles north of Downtown Saigon. Vietnam's hot season was beating down on us. Outside the temperature reached 100 degrees in the shade. The humidity was a solid 100 percent. My Mom let the window air conditioning units run full blast, but with so many of us in the room, it was hot and uncomfortable and all of us were sweating.

The bell rang downstairs. No one wanted to get up to answer the door. It could be another beggar or a desperate refugee from Central Vietnam pleading for food. So many of these folks had come around in recent days. Or maybe it was someone wanting to tell us more bad news. The bell rang again, beckoning. Finally I got up and ran down the stairs.

I opened the door and there in front of me was my dear old Dad. I jumped on him and hugged him with all of my might. He was much darker, his hair was longer and he had an inkling of a beard. It was obvious that he had not shaved, nor showered, for days or even months. He gave me a bear hug and smiled victoriously. He had made it home alive.

I held onto his hand and ran him up the steps yelling — *"Ba về tới rồi! Ba về tới rồi!"* Dad is home! Dad is home!

I was so happy that I was yelling at the top of my lungs with tears running down my face.

Mom met us at the top of the stairs with eyes wide-open in disbelief. She cried, she laughed and she hugged my Dad with the desperation of a woman who had transformed in an instant from despair to ecstasy. She thought he was dead, yet here he was. It was a miracle. Everyone in the room rushed to my Dad with hugs and kisses to welcome him back from the brink of death.

My Dad Trung-Tá Lê Công Chính in 1970

My Dad sought out Huy Hoàng and Hà, and held them tight. Elated, all of us kids surrounded him. We jumped up and down talking at the same time. We pulled and tugged on him to get his attention and laughed and hugged each other. Mom stood by smiling widely with tears streaming down her face. I had never seen my Mom so happy before and my heart was bursting with joy.

That was the happiest day of our lives in Vietnam.

My Uncles Cậu Năm and Dượng Bảy, my Mom's older brother and brother-in-law, respectively, came over the next day. They met with my Dad for a long time. We could hear raised voices and quiet whispers, and there were intense negotiations.

Cậu Năm's Family in Nha Trang in early 1970

Dì Bảy's Family in Nha Trang in 1975

My Dad, a career Army officer, wanted to re-enlist, go to Xuân Lộc and fight. He talked Dượng Bảy, who was also an officer, into doing the same thing; but Cậu Năm, who was a career bureaucrat was not about to let them do so. Cậu Năm had just given up everything he had owned, all the relatives in Nha Trang, all the things that he knew and loved to evacuate his family to Saigon; and now he wanted to flee the country. He knew the fighting was over, and the South had lost. He pleaded with my Dad to listen to him, listen with his brain and not with his heart. The debates went on for hours, and finally Cậu Năm stormed out of the room. He called on my Mom and Dì Bảy to reason with my Dad.

My Mom wept and begged my Dad to hear what Cậu Năm had to say. *"Anh nên nghe lời Anh Năm. Giờ này mà còn ghi tên đi đánh giặc chi nữa? Tụi Mỹ đã bỏ Việt Nam rồi thì mình còn làm gì được?"* You should listen to Anh Năm. What good is it now to re-enlist? The Americans have abandoned Vietnam, what can we do now?

My Dad replied, trying to convince everyone that there was still hope. *"Nếu mình giữ được Xuân Lộc thì Sài Gòn sẽ không mất đâu. Anh sẽ trở về sau khi đẩy lui tụi Việt Cộng."* If we can hold on to Xuân Lộc, Saigon will be safe. I will return home after we push back the Việt Cộng.

My mom begged him. *"Không có vũ khí và tiếp liệu thì làm sao mà đánh được. Anh nên ở nhà lo kiếm cách chạy đi là tốt nhất."* Without ammunition and logistical support, how can you fight? You best stay here and help us plan our departure.

She started to cry and my Dad held her and slowly wiped away her tears. He said, *"Nếu mất nước thì gia đình mình sẽ tan rả. Tụi Việt Cộng sẽ giết chết Anh. Anh Năm, Dượng Bảy và có thể cả Hùng nữa. Anh phải hy sinh để chận lại tụi gian ác này."* If we lose the war, our family will be destroyed. They will kill me, Anh Năm, Dượng Bảy and possibly Hùng as well. Therefore I must stop these vicious people now.

My Mom cried even louder now. *"Anh đi thì Anh sẽ chết một mình. Tại sao Anh không chịu ở lại. Dù sao đi nữa, nếu có chết, thì mình sẽ chết chung với nhau."* If you go, you will die by yourself. Why don't you stay? So if we die, at least we can die together.

Now it was my Dad's turn to cry. *"Anh sẽ không bị sao đâu. Em ở lại lo cho tụi con mình. Nếu Anh có bị gì đi nữa thì tụi nhỏ sẽ biết rằng Ba chúng nó đã hy sinh bảo vệ chúng nó đến giây phút cuối cùng."* I will be all right. Take care of our kids. And if anything happens to me, they should know that I tried to protect them until my very last breath.

All of us kids started to cry. We were so scared, and my Mom knew this time he would not come back to us. She held onto him tightly, as we all wrapped our arms around them, crying. Our cousins and the other adults were in tears as well.

After what seemed like forever, my Mom sat down on the chair. Tears streaming down her face, she did not know what else to say. Many times before, she had begged him not to go to the front line, but she could never stop him. His patriotic duty and love for country were more than the love he bore for his family. Time and time again, he returned wounded on a stretcher, and she had nursed him back to health while he spent weeks in the military hospital, only to see him off to war again.

To our astonishment, my Mom reached for his handgun lying on the table. She cocked the trigger and placed the nozzle against her temple.

"Em sẽ tự tử bây giờ cho Anh đi một mình." I will kill myself right now so you may go.

We all cried out loudly, *"Má, Má đừng làm như vậy."* Mom, Mom, please don't do it.

Anh Hùng and Chị Lêvi ran to her, imploring her to stop.

My Dad kneeled down by her feet with tears running down his face. He embraced her and softly said, *"Em bỏ súng xuống đi. Anh sẽ không đi đâu."* Please put down the gun. I will not go.

My Mom put the gun on the table and held my Dad. We put our arms around them and wept.

That was how the war ended for my Dad. After twenty-five-years of service for his country, his final battle was for his family.

CHAPTER TWO

My Father's War

*"Let every nation know, whether it wishes us well or ill,
that we shall pay any price, bear any burden,
meet any hardship, support any friend, oppose any foe,
in order to assure the survival and the success of liberty"*
— US President John F. Kennedy
on his Inauguration Day, Jan. 20, 1961

*"The United States did not keep its promise
to help us fight for freedom, and it was in the same fight that the
United States lost 50,000 of its young men."*
— Vietnam President Nguyễn Văn Thiệu
on his resignation day, April 21, 1975

Vietnam is a small country located in Southeast Asia. It is slightly smaller than California and consists of mostly hills and densely forested mountains in the North and Central areas. The most fertile flatlands are located in the south along the Mekong River. The Highlands of Vietnam start south of the City of Dalat and run up through the north into China. During the winter months between November and April (dry season), the monsoon winds from China blow down along the coast and bring considerable moisture into Vietnam's Central Highlands. In the summer months (wet season), heavy torrential rains from the South China Sea bring even more moisture to the Highlands as well as to the entire country.

Located in the hills and mountains of the Central Highlands, the provincial towns of Kontum and Pleiku of South Vietnam were always cold and wet. During the last century, most Vietnamese moved to the cities and left the land behind for the Montagnards, who lived in tribes throughout these areas. They made their living off the land by farming and hunting wild game. They loved the land and tolerated the weather.

On January 13, 1975, the hills and mountains were covered with low cloud and heavy fog. My Dad had served in these hills and mountains with the Second Corps for more than a year. He wanted out and had requested his commander to give him another assignment elsewhere. He did not quite understand why, but he knew that he wanted to go farther north to serve in the First Corps near the DMZ. If the country was to fall, he wanted to be there at the front line defending her. Months before, he had submitted the request for reassignment, and on this day Colonel Phạm Duy Tất, the Brigade Commander of South Vietnam's Second Corps, signed the order to send my Dad to the First Corps's front line near Danang.

The Huey helicopter lifted off from the Second Corps Central Command Center amid the heavy fog with my Dad and his single backpack as the lone passenger. He leaned back on the bench seat and thought about his past missions. Ever since the Geneva Convention of 1954, when the French established the Army of the Republic of Vietnam (ARVN), he had been a Lieutenant in the Armed Forces. And he had risked his life on a daily basis for this war-torn country. He had his fair share of getting shot at and had long forgotten how many times he had been wounded.

The altitude and the soggy weather caused discomfort in his back, where he was shot several years before. He recalled the search-and-destroy mission of that evening when his company was ambushed by a full regiment of NVA. His outnumbered and outgunned company dug in and put up a fight, but as the sky got darker, he had no choice but to retreat when they began to run out of ammunition.

The red tracers from the enemy lit up the air and ground all around them and many of his men were shot. He called for backup, but there was no air support. His other Marine Amphibious units were on the way, but still too far away. The soldier next to him got a bullet from an AK-47 right through his left arm and the man went down hard as blood spurted from his wound. When my Dad bent down to pick up the wounded soldier, a bullet hit his metal helmet and spun it off his head.

The force was tremendous, as though he was hit on the head with a sledgehammer. His neck throbbed severely and his vision blurred. It took him several long seconds to regain his orientation. No longer protected by the helmet, he crawled to the wounded soldier, grabbed him and carried him away from the deadly fire. He could tell that his reserve units had finally arrived as red tracers jetted back toward the other side.

He laid the wounded soldier down to catch his breath and that's when the flak jacket exposed him, and a bullet burned its way through his right lower back. He passed out and didn't wake up until several days later in a regional hospital, his midsection wrapped under layers of bandages.

More than half of his company was killed in the jungle attack. He hated war and he despised the Communists for destroying his men. The General gave him a Purple Heart medal and a month off to spend with his family. After that, he was wounded several more times, but none as severe.

He told me that it was the will of God that he survived. Sitting back on the bench of the helicopter, he wondered how God had protected and guided him throughout his years of combat. Having served in the dangerous hills and mountains of Kontum and Pleiku, he thanked God everyday for keeping him alive in such a hostile environment.

Kontum and Pleiku were strategically important for South Vietnam. Their hills contained the main military supply corridors for all of Central Vietnam including cities, towns and seaports. Pleiku was located on the central plateau, between Kontum in the north, and Ban Mê Thuột to the south. This made Pleiku the main center of defense for Vietnam's highland region and both sides of the war were well aware of its strategic significance. The NVA constantly bombarded the towns with heavy artillery and assaulted the ARVN regularly.

For the soldiers of Kontum and Pleiku, there was never any rest. And for the civilians, life was hell. There were days that the Communists shelled the town nonstop, followed by days of eerie silence. People got frightened on those quiet days, as they knew the NVA were regrouping and another wave of attacks would soon begin. When the attacks came, many innocent civilians were killed and wounded. People locked themselves inside their houses and hunkered down in an inside room where sandbags were stacked high along the walls. Many had fled the towns, but others had nowhere else to go since things were bad all over the country.

My Dad had lived through so many cat-and-mouse attacks, as he called them. The Communists persistently put pressure on the ARVN, but would not dare make a frontal attack. South Vietnamese Marines and Rangers had always pushed them back and killed and wounded many of their soldiers each time they conducted major offensives. In recent days, small attacks had grown into major attacks, where hundreds of NVA soldiers invaded parts of the territory and held them for a long duration. The Marines and Rangers had to fight them more aggressively and our side started to suffer more casualties.

My Dad had had enough of the frustrating mountain warfare, and he wanted to move on. He had volunteered to go to the front line and had declined several good offers of promotion. One was to stay and to lead the Special Forces at Pleiku and the other was to become the Regiment Commander of Địa Phương Quân (local militia) of the Second Corps at Ban Mê Thuột. Both of these opportunities would give him the chance to lead his army against the enemy, but he chose to go to the DMZ instead. Now he was about to go farther north to Danang, South Vietnam's northernmost major city. He prayed that God would be with him this time, as He had been so many times before.

His mission was to hold the enemy at the DMZ as long as possible, which would give refugees time to evacuate South Vietnam's rugged Central Highlands, a mission that would require supreme sacrifice, but one that could save thousands of innocent lives. It was the mission that he trained for all his life, and it was the mission that he wanted. He prayed for success.

On January 26, 1975, General Ngô Quang Trưởng, the Chief Commander of the First Corps with the Central Command based in Danang, executed the order to make my Dad the Commander of the 913th Infantry Regiment composed of three full battalions of more than 5,000 armed men. On that day, my Dad had become the highest ranking army officer in charge of defending South Vietnam's northern most front line. And his job was to hold onto Quảng Trị at all costs.

Quảng Trị was a small outpost along the east bank of Thạch Hản River less than twenty miles from the DMZ. It was situated on the national coastal highway called Highway 1, and it lay between provincial roads 560 on the west and 555 on the east. The road network of north-south and east-west corridors passed through Quảng Trị. The City stood like a miniature of Huế with its own citadel. More importantly, Quảng Trị was located only forty-five miles north of Huế, a historically significant town where the royal families of Vietnam used to live.

The town of Quảng Trị (the same name as the province) was built on the coastal plane, and vulnerable to attack from all directions. It had changed hands many times between the NVA and the South Vietnamese ARVN during the long war. The Communists as well as the Americans expected the supposedly unmotivated, poorly equipped South Vietnamese soldiers who were defending the city of Quảng Trị to just melt away. Instead, the brave men of the ARVN stayed, fought and held the city, battle after battle. As the new commander, my Dad wanted to continue this military tradition. He wanted to hold his ground and give the Communists a good fight. Quảng Trị was my Dad's new home by choice, and he intended to defend it with all he had.

My Dad received his orders from General Ngô Quang Trưởng, a young, tall, homely-looking Lieutenant General who was well known and well respected by his men and the people of South Vietnam.

US General Norman Schwarzkopf stated in his autobiography, *It Doesn't Take A Hero*, that "His face was pinched and intense, not at all handsome. Yet he was revered by his officers and troops—and feared by those North Vietnamese commanders who knew of his ability ... General Trưởng was the most brilliant tactical commander I'd ever known."

My Dad boarded another Huey helicopter heading north. It was early in the morning and the sun had just risen from behind the mountains. Looking out the wide-open doors of the Huey, he could see the majestic Đèo Hải Vân (Hai Van Hills) in the distance. On the south side, Danang was clearly visible under the rising sun; on the north side, the City of Huế was still covered by a dense fog.

My Dad told me about how the helicopter turned sharply toward the sea to avoid sniper fire. Continuing north, it kept a safe distance from the shoreline. As it approached Quảng Trị, my Dad could see thousands of empty houses and huts of citizens that had already fled the town. The battles of the summer of 1972 had destroyed much of the city and left it just about empty. Since then, some residents had come back and found their houses in ruins and unlivable, but they were determined to rebuild.

From the air, it was difficult to tell which houses were newly rebuilt and which ones were abandoned, as none of them seemed finished. The helicopter circled twice and landed at Quảng Trị's modest command post. The post was a collection of Quonset huts, prefabricated shelters having a semicircular arching roof of corrugated metal, hurriedly rebuilt by the ARVN after the Communists had leveled it a couple years earlier. It stood defiantly as a symbol of the undying valor of the South Vietnamese Army.

Lieutenant Colonel Đỗ Kỳ, the Provincial Governor, welcomed my Dad with open arms. He had heard about my Dad's fearless reputation and was glad to see him. The governor was a short, stocky man with a northern accent. Like many others in the forces, he was very superstitious and had already picked out a date to introduce my Dad to his new battalions and assume his new role. He believed that by picking an auspicious date, it would give my Dad the good fortune he needed to lead our troops to victory. Not being a superstitious man, my Dad would have preferred air support instead, but he went along with Lieutenant Colonel Đỗ Kỳ. It was his show, for now.

After having lunch with the governor at the base, my Dad took a tour of the town. The city of Quảng Trị had changed dramatically from my Dad's last visit fourteen years before. What once was a booming commercial town had now been reduced to a collection of temporary housing and huts made of aluminum corrugated panels provided by the South Vietnamese Government. The allocation was ten sheets of these long corrugated panels per family. At one time, there were more than 200,000 people living here surviving on government food rations. Since then, many had left to go to Huế. Outside these camps were several modest churches and social service offices made of the same temporary corrugated aluminum sheets. At night, the cold winds blew down from the mountains and made the huts bitterly cold. During the day, the baking sun turned the huts into ovens, making it impossible for people to stay inside. Yet this was all the people of Quảng Trị had.

My Dad made his way to the Church of Lavang near the center of town. It used to be a glorious church, revered by all, where many miracles had taken place, but the battles of 1972 had damaged most of it. The religious people of Quảng Trị had tried to rebuild the church only to have it blasted again in recent fighting. The roof had caved in, and of the four walls, only the one behind the altar was partially standing. Somehow the serene statue of Mother Mary of Lavang still stood there humbly, unharmed, among the ruins. My Dad told me that he kneeled down before the statue and said a prayer for himself, his family and his homeland.

Fourteen years before, he visited this church with my Mom, who was pregnant at the time. Back then he prayed for a son who would preach God's good news and bring joy to people. Just as every devout Catholic Vietnamese man hoped, he wanted to have a son that he could give to the Church. He wanted a priest in the family. When my Mom kneeled down beside my Dad before the statue, the baby leaped in her womb. My Mom lightly took my Dad's hand and placed it on her swollen belly. Feeling happy that the baby was kicking, my Dad named the baby "Vui" for Vui Mừng (Happiness) and gave him the patron saint name of John the Baptist, who, according to the Bible, had leaped with joy in Elizabeth's womb when Mother Mary visited her.

That was a joyful time, unlike this day in 1975 when war was ravaging everything, and the church, like my Dad, bore wounds and scars. He told me that he silently prayed to Mother Mary in thanksgiving, as his fourteen-year-old son was now attending a seminary called An-Phong Học-Viện in Thủ Đức and he had fulfilled his promise to give a child to the Church. He prayed that Mother Mary would watch over his son, Vui.

He left the church and went to the citadel. The Citadel Đinh Công Tráng, a scenic town perched on the bank of Thạch Hản River, had become nothing more than a pile of loose bricks and twisted metal. The nearby buildings were in no better shape; everything was shattered by the war. The two bridges that connected the highways to the town lay twisted in the river. Suddenly my Dad recalled the verses of a poem he had long forgotten:

"Thế hệ tôi làm nhơ trang liệt sữ,
Một giòng sông một chứng tích tương tàn."

My generation soiled up history,
A river a devastated evidence.

My Dad stood there with his Army Rangers looking across the river at his enemies holding guns, staring back. The fighting would resume soon enough.

Tết (Vietnamese New Year) was just around the corner, and rumor had it that the Việt Cộng would take advantage of the holidays to launch another major offensive. Catholic Bishop Nguyễn Văn Thuận of the Diocese of Nha Trang, who had just visited Lavang, had urged his priests to ask the congregations to migrate far south toward Phan Rang to escape the carnage that was inevitable. Many took their advice and left; others abandoned their rebuilding efforts and just sat in the ruins and awaited their fate.

Tết Ất Mảo, February 11, 1975 …

It was the Year of the Cat, and it reminded my Dad of the time he was the Mayor of Tân Châu District in the deep south of Vietnam. Dượng Năm, the brother-in-law of Hòa Hảo Supreme Spiritual Leader Huỳnh Phú Sổ, led a popular religious sect there, and liked to tell people of Huỳnh Phú Sổ's prophecy:

> *"Mèo kêu bá tánh lao xao,*
> *Đến khi Rồng Rắn máu đào chỉnh ghê,*
> *Con ngựa lại đá con dê,*
> *Khắp trong trần hạ nhiều bề lao đao,*
> *Khỉ kia cũng bị xáo xào,*
> *Canh khuya gà gáy máu đào mới ngưng."*

The prophecy called for seven years of bloodshed starting with the Year of the Cat. While my Dad never placed much faith in prophecies, he witnessed the fierce fighting at Ban Mê Thuột, Pleiku and Kontum, and wondered what the future held.

On New Year's Eve, special envoys of senators and other representatives of South Vietnam's government visited the front line and offered customary gifts of cash, radios, watches and cigarettes to the soldiers. In a private conversation, my Dad learned that the government had just arrested thirteen Communist infiltrators working undercover as senior-level news reporters in Saigon.

My Dad said that their mischief and misinformation created uncertainty in the minds of the people, convincing them that the war was now in its final stage and the Americans had given up. Many citizens believed the propaganda and became frightened, and that set off a chain of rumors that caused the people to lose touch with reality. As soldiers, my Dad and his men could readily deal with the effects of warfare, but they were not prepared for the psychological chaos in the capitol, fed by lies and fear.

That night my Dad put his forces on high alert, and they stayed up all night, ready for a brutal attack. The cold night air plus the dread of impending battle made my Dad and his troops jumpy and trigger happy. At the time, North Vietnam was one hour ahead of South

Vietnam. When the clock struck the North's midnight, their hearts pounded and their breathing came in short gasps in anticipation of bloodshed and mayhem. As they lay anxiously in their freshly dug trenches along the river, they all felt they might not live to celebrate the next New Year with their families. When the South's midnight came and went without incident, my Dad and his forces kept alert and ready just in case. When the sun rose behind the mountains, they finally relaxed.

My Dad went to church early in the morning on New Year's Day, as he had done for years. He then gathered his troops to raise the South Vietnamese flag and to sing our national anthem in celebration of the New Year. Afterwards, they exchanged usual New Year's wishes of good luck, good health and wealth. General Ngô Quang Trưởng paid them a surprise visit and said he was very pleased with the good job my Dad had done in keeping the troops equipped, ready and in good spirits.

Then it was my Dad's turn to visit the soldiers of his companies, batteries and battalions. The air was cold, the red clay was wet, the misty rain continued throughout the day. On the hills, the vegetation had turned deep green with the promise of beautiful spring flowers to come. Exuding confidence as he extended well wishes to his soldiers, my Dad prayed silently that all would make it through the next three days of the Tết holidays. Fortunately, they did, but the hour of calamity was soon in coming.

Less than three weeks after Tết, on March 1, the North Vietnamese Army assaulted on all fronts with a heavy barrage of artillery shells and blasts from T-54 and PT-76 tanks. For days, the rain of mortar shells chipped away at the men of the 913th Infantry Regiment. Many had died and were wounded, but despite the heavy casualties, they hung on. My Dad requested air support, but this time there were no F-5s and Phantom aircraft to the rescue.

The NVA had launched massive attacks throughout the Central Highlands. With extremely limited resources, only strategic and high value battles got air support from the South Vietnamese Air Force. The American Air Force and Navy were ordered to stand down and not to intervene, and the battles throughout the Central Highlands became a mass slaughter. My Dad called for air evacuation of wounded soldiers and civilians, but his calls went unanswered. Thousands of South Vietnamese soldiers and innocent civilians died, but my Dad and his men dug in and refused to retreat.

To make matters worse, at midnight on March 6, the Communists blew up the only bridge connecting Quảng Trị and Huế and completely cut off all supply routes to town. Never giving up easily, my Dad and the men of the 913th Regiment and 110th Regiment continued to block the NVA advances. The NVA attacked Quảng Trị in wave after wave of infantry backed by T-54 tanks and heavy artillery, but each time, my Dad's courageous men pushed them back to the north side of the river. The battles raged on for days with death tolls on both sides rising rapidly.

Then on March 10, the 320th Division of the North Vietnamese Army (NVA) launched a major attack on Ban Mê Thuột, an important strategic outpost, to begin the full-blown invasion of South Vietnam. Well-equipped NVA backed by heavy artillery and tanks easily overwhelmed the meagerly defended Army of the Republic of Vietnam (ARVN) at Ban Mê Thuột. From that day forward, the Central Highlands of South Vietnam were under constant bombardment, and explosions and machine gun fire filled the air. Despite the vicious barrage, my Dad and his men held their position.

Soon Ban Mê Thuột fell, and South Vietnam President Nguyễn Văn Thiệu was forced to order the troops in Pleiku and all other command posts in the Central Highlands to retreat. The ARVN forces fled down the ill-maintained tertiary road LTL-7B through Cheo Reo to Tuy Hòa, joining thousands of civilians trying to escape. The NVA attacked ferociously, raining artillery down on the soldiers and refugees from positions high in the hills. Lacking munitions, the South Vietnamese Air Force could do nothing to stop the massacre of convoys and innocent people below, and more than one hundred thousand evacuees from the Pleiku and Kontum areas were killed or stranded.

My Dad told me that there were plenty of bombs and munitions at our airbases in Danang, Phan Rang, and Biên Hoà, but the Americans would not release the trigger mechanisms needed to activate these weapons. To the Americans, the War had ended.

As the NVA advanced into villages and towns, people from all over the region hurried southbound along Highway 1 in mass confusion. As Kontum and Pleiku fell, thousands of men, women, children, and soldiers jammed the roads. Many died in stampedes, and many more could not cope with the cold, damp and hunger as they wound through the treacherous forest, and fell by the side of the road.

Although my Dad was not caught up in the evacuation, his situation was just as grim. He and his troops were trapped farther north near the DMZ in the ghost town of Quảng Trị. Across the river to the north, the NVA was attacking and shelling day and night. After conquering Kontum and Pleiku in the south, the NVA was making its way toward Danang and Huế. Knowing the evacuation route had been cut off, my Dad and his men continued to stand their ground.

On March 14th, the ARVN Central Command ordered Dad to retreat from the City of Quảng Trị to Danang. My Dad's 913th Infantry Regiment was to be the last to leave. His men had fought and died valiantly, but now he had to withdraw to protect whatever was left of his forces. The NVA continued to shower them with mortar rounds and advance ever closer to his position.

On March 18, ARVN Corps I Central Command retreated from Huế to Danang, but the Communists advanced with astonishing speed. Their heavy artillery blasted the villages and towns, while battalions and tanks rolled north of Mỹ Chánh River, burning houses and indiscriminately murdering villagers. At 7 o'clock that evening, when the last soldier had crossed Trường Phước Bridge, my Dad ordered his troops to blow up the bridge to slow down the NVA's advance. As he stood on the south side of the river looking back at Lavang Church, he said a prayer and a goodbye to Mother Mary while thanking Her for his blessed protection.

South Vietnamese soldiers had died by the thousands in this retreat, but the generals wanted my Dad to keep constant pressure on the NVA and continue to slow down their advance. They gave him the commands of additional forces from the 120th and 121st Battalions plus heavy artillery. The goal was to protect the evacuation of the people of Central Vietnam and make the VC pay for every inch of ground they took with their own blood.

He positioned his troops sparingly along the ten miles of Mỹ Chánh River and pounded the enemy on the other side of the river with heavy artillery. For four long days, the battle went on with each side suffering massive losses. More than two thousand of his men had died on the south bank of the river, and possibly more on the other side. Everywhere bodies of soldiers piled up along the trenches. The screams of wounded soldiers could be heard throughout the battlefront. Medical supplies were scarce. As ammunition was running short, soldiers defended their positions with M-16 and AR-15 rifles dropped by their fallen comrades.

On my Dad's side of the river, there was no more food and no additional supplies. The monsoon rains had started to fill up the trenches like small rivers. His men were hungry, cold and wet. They had no rest for days, and their morale was low. But together they held the line against the enemy.

General Lâm Quang Thi, a young southern man who had graduated from the same National Military Academy as my Dad, visited the front line and complimented the bravery of my Dad's men. The General also informed my Dad that most of the people of Huế had evacuated to Danang and that it was time to withdraw. My Dad hurriedly dispatched his trusted friend Major Đỗ Thiên Phanh to Huế to send a telegram back home to my Mom notifying her that my Dad had withdrawn from Quảng Trị and to pray for him and his troops.

During the night of Sunday, March 23, my Dad ordered his troops to withdraw from Mỹ Chánh to An Lỗ, more than twenty miles away. Thousands of exhausted men marched quietly under the cover of darkness and in heavy rain carrying soaked backpacks while assisting the wounded. No convoy of trucks, no helicopters, no tanks helped them. Just the sheer will to survive. The monsoon rains added insult to the pain of the retreating soldiers, yet that night my Dad had successfully withdrawn his men without further bloodshed or loss of life.

However, as the NVA were closing in on them, my Dad and his troops could not stop and rest in An Lỗ and kept moving. For three weeks, the NVA had been held back by the 913th Infantry Regiment and 110th Ranger Regiment of the South Vietnamese Army, and they were not about to let their adversaries escape. Like a lion out of its cage, the NVA ferociously attacked the retreating troops and An Lỗ fell at 6:30 on the evening of March 24.

The NVA advanced so quickly my Dad's troops could no longer use long range munitions because the enemy was simply too close, so he ordered all cannons and heavy artillery destroyed to prevent the Communists from seizing them and using them against them as they fled.

He then ordered all functional tanks to head toward the historic city of Huế as quickly as possible. Encouraged by the lack of return fire and minimal resistance, the NVA forces quickly captured Huế, burned it down and massacred many of its citizens. Captured South Vietnamese soldiers were killed without mercy.

At 9 o'clock in the evening, Huế was deserted, as civilians and soldiers, most wearing civilian clothing, were trying to get to Thuận An Bay. Earlier, the segment of Highway 1 running from Huế to Danang had fallen and was under Communist control. The people of Huế and those from Northern provinces had nowhere else to go, except out to sea. Thuận An Bay was their last hope.

Thuận An Bay was located east of Huế, and the road to Thuận An had become a gigantic bottleneck, jammed solidly with desperate people fleeing the advancing enemy. Cars, trucks, and mopeds that were out of gas piled up on both sides of the road next to household goods that were thrown away by the exhausted refugees, who could not carry them anymore. Many vehicles were on fire, and gunfire and explosions from grenades could be heard everywhere. Heavily armed soldiers, in and out of uniform, forced their way through the crowd. A young soldier reported to my Dad that he saw Lt. Colonel Kỳ and Lt. Colonel Nhiễm swim across the bay to the ferry on the other side earlier that evening.

That was the end. The command structure of the South Vietnamese Armed Forces of the First Corps had dissolved. The only way out was to swim across the bay and try to find a way back to Danang. As the last act of a commander, my Dad used the communicator in his Jeep and called the commanders of his three battalions to inform them of the only way out. These were short calls, difficult and direct, but they were necessary to save lives. He then destroyed the communicator before he ran out onto the beach. He knew that even if he were to die that night, he had tried his best to save as many people as he could. He then prayed that God would forgive him for his failings and guide him to safety. He thought of his family and wished we could be reunited in peace.

The Road to Thuận An Bay

My Dad told me that it was 2 o'clock in the morning on March 25 when he stripped down to his shorts and dove into the cold dark water of the South China Sea. Using inner tubes from the tires of cars and trucks to keep afloat, he and dozens of his men swam for hours in the frigid water toward the east side of Thuận An Bay. As the bay was wide, the current strong and the water very cold, they kept each other alive by talking and telling each other not to waste energy. They swam in the dark and somehow made it to the other side.

After landing on the beach, many men ran to the villages to use the main roads, but my Dad and a group of ten men raced along the beach toward Danang. In the early hours of the morning, they came upon a small fishing village and found a small fishing boat that seemed to be in good shape with ample fuel. As they pushed the small boat out to sea, the owner, an old fisherman, rushed out from the village to stop them. The men forced the fisherman to go with them. And lucky for them that they did.

The waves were high and crashing down hard, but the expert old man masterfully navigated the boat that was overloaded with troops. The small outboard engine sputtered and ran to everyone's relief and the boat slowly moved toward Danang. The morning sun shone gloriously over the crystal blue water, and the north winds quickly warmed their spirits. My Dad and his men had lived another day.

After eight hours at sea, they arrived at Danang in the afternoon. Danang was one of the largest cities in Central Vietnam with mountains on one side and the South China Sea on the other, and was one of the country's most important ports. The US established both an airbase and a seaport near Non Nước Beach to provide logistical support for Central Vietnam. Non Nước Beach was a white sandy beach on the outskirts of Danang and was renowned for both its spectacular beauty and for its history as an R&R destination for American troops during the war.

When my Dad landed with his men, Non Nước Beach was filled with people from small fishing boats and large cargo ships that came in from other northern towns. The US airbase had been evacuated and now became a large camp of refugees from Quảng Trị and Huế. The naval base was so full of people that South Vietnam naval ships could not dock to load or unload for fear that the mass of refugees would charge them, try to scramble aboard and overwhelm the crews. The population of Danang had now swelled to more than a million people, mostly refugees.

None of his men wanted to report to Central Command; instead they went off to find their families in this sea of people. Alone, my Dad pushed his way through the crowd and made his way back to the Danang Officer's Club. Lieutenant Colonel Đặng Đình Kiền, a tall and skinny friend of my Dad, loaned him two sets of uniforms. They fitted him well, and in full uniform, he reported to the Central Command. Lieutenant Colonels Kỳ and Nhiễm had just arrived there as well.

The Central Command had mostly been evacuated according to the earlier order of President Nguyễn Văn Thiệu and now there was just a skeleton crew of civilians and high ranking officers working feverishly to burn critical intelligence documents and destroy equipment.

Two months earlier my Dad was here accepting his assignments from General Ngô Quang Trưởng and departed on a Huey helicopter; this time he came back on a highjacked fishing boat, half naked, reporting to a nearly empty headquarters. He was happy to be alive.

After the customary paperwork, he quickly said goodbye to his friends and rushed to the post office. After what seemed like hours standing in line, he finally sent home a message to my Mom and let her know that he had made it to Danang, and hoped that my Mom would get the telegram in Saigon. Then he went to a nearby church.

My Dad told me that the following four days were chaotic. The poor people of Central Vietnam had flooded the town. To the north and the west, the Communist forces were bearing down, and all roads southbound were cut off, as the NVA had taken control of Pleiku, Kontum and Ban Mê Thuột. The only way out was by sea, but all the large ships and boats had left port. In the distance, the ships of the South Vietnamese Navy were waiting but did not dare come in to dock, so people shuttled back and forth on small fishing boats, risking their lives against the massive waves of the South China Sea.

Several smaller naval vessels motored in closer to the beach and when that happened, people lashed together inner tubes and set out to reach them. Hundreds and hundreds of the strongest people, mostly soldiers, flailed the water with paddles and their arms and reached the safety of the naval ships. When they hoisted themselves onboard, there wasn't even room to sit, as thousands of people were already there.

On shore, thousands more watched for many days and nights, hoping that someone would come in and carry them to safety. On the outskirts of town, the NVA and their tanks were closing in. This time they did not bother to use their heavy artillery. The South Vietnamese Army had disappeared into the population, and the only resistance came from cars and trucks clogging the roads.

At 5 o'clock in the morning of Saturday, March 29, General Ngô Quang Trưởng, Lieutenant Colonels Kỳ, Nhiễm and my Dad silently drifted over to the far end of the former naval base. A naval personnel landing ship with the hull number LSM-404 Hương Giang quietly landed on the beach and dropped its landing ramp onto the sand. The four men and a small crowd rushed in from the darkness, and the ship quickly backed away from the beach.

By 10 o'clock that morning, the NVA had completely taken Danang. Their flag of the lone yellow star on the red banner was raised on the pole at the center of the former ARVN Command Center. From a distance, the convoy of South Vietnamese ships slowly headed south. On the empty beach, the high waves pounded the crystal white sand, and the heavy rain started to wash away the millions of footprints left by desperate people.

My Dad prayed quietly as he stood staring at the shore, wiping away tears. May God protect the poor people of Central Vietnam.

CHAPTER THREE

Exodus

Vietnam was a country of no consequence.

For thousands of years, the Chinese in the North had tried time and again to annex the land of Vietnam into Greater China. Each time they failed, not because they could not win a battle or a war, but because they always came to the conclusion that Vietnam was not worth the effort. Vietnam had no significant natural resources, and the Vietnamese people were incompliant, unlike the traditional Chinese, and preferred to fight the Chinese for every tree and blade of grass.

Then came the French. For a hundred years, the French were successful in conquering Vietnam. The French brought with them Christianity and gave the Vietnamese our written language. These two cultural contributions enabled the Vietnamese to open up to the world and acclimate easily into Western and other cultures and allowed us to learn Latin-based languages more quickly than people from other Asian countries. For years, the coexistence with the French proved more and more comfortable, and the Vietnamese people conveniently overlooked the fact that they were a colony for a foreign power and source of wealth for the French Empire.

World War I and World War II changed all that. Aware of the weakened power of the French Empire, factions of Vietnamese started to dream about a land of independence, free from French laws and influence.

Hồ Chí Minh took advantage of this nationalistic sentiment and mobilized the people in northern Vietnam to fight the French. During this period, the French were focused on rebuilding their own country ravaged by the Germans during World War II, and they just wanted their forces in Vietnam to go back to France. With support from Communist China, Hồ Chí Minh and his forces, (called Việt Minh), beat the French at the final battle in 1954 staged at Điện Biên Phủ, not because of the might of the Vietnamese people, but because of the French Empire's lack of will.

The situation back then, while serious and even heroic, reminded me of an innocent TV commercial. Two children's soccer teams: one celebrated its victory, and the other pained its loss. While the winners held their trophy high, the losers got McDonalds for lunch. The winners went away hungry. The losers went home happy.

Hồ Chí Minh and his forces had beaten the French magnificently, but they had not won the *real* war. The prize they wanted the most was un-winnable, and that prize was the hearts and souls of the Vietnamese people, especially the people of South Vietnam.

Around 1950, the United States of America started sending "advisors" to Vietnam. Using the lame excuse of helping its ally, the French, America got involved in Vietnam to satisfy its arrogance. The American people, riding a national high from their military victories in Europe and Asia, wanted to play big brother for the French in Vietnam.

The US and France worked out a deal with Hồ Chí Minh and his Việt Minh Forces to divide Vietnam into north and south using the seventeenth parallel as the dividing Demilitarized Zone (DMZ). It was meant to be a temporary partition designed to enable the French to save face and withdraw from Vietnam in an orderly manner. But the Americans had another idea: a permanently divided Vietnam. That would let the US contain the expansion of communism into Southeast Asia, similar to how the US and the Soviet Union divided North and South Korea, with communism in the north and a budding republic in the south. So the Americans got involved and stayed for more than twenty-five years.

In 1965, the war began in earnest, and as the body count of courageous American soldiers grew higher, the American people, like the French, lost interest in Vietnam. A new generation of baby-boomers, who did not want to die in foreign wars their parents had started, demanded that American forces withdraw from Vietnam.

During the Vietnamese New Year's celebration of Tết Mậu Thân in 1968, Communist North Vietnam, with the full support of Communist China and Russia, attacked the South with massive forces that spread throughout South Vietnam. The goal of Hồ Chí Minh was to take over South Vietnam by force in one huge battle, but his army was soundly defeated by the South Vietnamese Army, supported by the US.

The VC tried again during the summer of 1972. This time, instead of spreading their forces throughout the South, they concentrated them and attacked three important provinces: Bình Long, Kontum and Quảng Trị. The battles were long and vicious and both sides suffered massive losses. Again the South Vietnamese Marines and Rangers heroically pushed back the enemy.

In the same year, US President Richard Nixon made peace with China, and the Vietnam War was over in the eyes of the Cold War enemies, namely China, Russia and the United States. However, on the ground in Vietnam, China and Russia continued to push the North Vietnamese to force its Communist doctrine onto the people of South Vietnam. As the Americans began their withdrawal from Vietnam, the words of President John F. Kennedy became meaningless:

"We shall ... support any friend, oppose any foe ..."

Earlier in 1975, while fully aware that the Americans were going to abandon them, South Vietnam's President Nguyễn Văn Thiệu took a gamble and sent a huge number of South Vietnamese Armed Forces to the front line just south of the DMZ; my Dad was one of the commanders in this last ditch effort. Everyone in the South was hoping that this action would stop the North Vietnamese advance.

Unlike the battles during the summer of 1972, when US B-52 bombers dropped tons of napalm onto the Hồ Chí Minh Trail in Laos and Cambodia and forced the Communists to withdraw from Central Vietnam, this time the Vietnamese Army fought alone without air support. The Americans did not even give the South Vietnamese helicopters to evacuate the wounded. The means to deliver ammunition and heavy artillery were brought to a standstill due to the lack of fuel for transport. The betrayal by the Americans and President Nguyễn Văn Thiệu's gamble failed the people of South Vietnam miserably and cost thousands of lives.

And it emboldened the North Vietnamese to accelerate their reunification efforts. They quickly overran South Vietnam's northern cities, such as Quảng Trị, Huế, and Đà Nẵng. The communist forces pressed forward and quickly captured Qui Nhơn and Nha Trang. There was no one left to stop or even to slow them down. In early April 1975, The Communist forces were at the edge of Xuân Lộc and Biên Hòa and only miles from Saigon.

On April 10, the US Congress declined to pass an emergency aid package supported by US President Gerald Ford to save South Vietnam. Instead, the US Congress forced President Ford to evacuate all American personnel from Vietnam within two weeks.

Exhausted by years of fighting, tired of massive government corruption and angered by the US abandonment, the people of South Vietnam lost the will to fight. Soldiers deserted their posts in massive numbers and joined the enormous convoy of refugees from Central Vietnam heading toward Saigon. Before long, the city was so congested that people started to live in makeshift tents throughout the city, and living conditions worsened daily.

On the evening of Monday, April 21, 1975, the President and Commander-in-Chief of South Vietnam, Nguyễn Văn Thiệu, resigned and turned power over to an interim government. His tearful resignation did little to comfort the people of South Vietnam, and it left the City in a state of disorder and fear. Refugees and citizens had nowhere else to go and were trapped in a dangerously overcrowded city. People swarmed the airport and harbors, and then the North Vietnamese heavy artillery started to rain down on the crammed city, setting buildings on fire and killing at random. Panic spread quickly as the bodies of innocent citizens piled up on the streets and at the hospitals.

Desperate and hopeless, many South Vietnamese leaders and soldiers killed themselves in public places such as shrines and temples. Such actions added to the people's anxiety and pushed South Vietnam to the brink of collapse.

Việt Cộng entered Tân Sơn Nhất Airport

During the days that followed the resignation of Nguyễn Văn Thiệu, convoys of American GMC trucks and Jeeps shuttled back and forth, taking Americans and other foreigners to safe havens. Dazed and confused, people in the street watched the movement; they huddled around their radios and TVs to listen to the constant government chatter trying to calm everybody down. Many others rushed home to be with their families. Some gathered at churches and temples, while many people followed the Americans to find shelter at the US and other foreign embassies, the airport, airbases, and seaports.

At home, my Dad sank down into the sofa, speechless, as he watched news of the President's resignation on TV. Next to him, Cậu Năm and Dượng Bảy were equally astonished.

These three men in their early forties had given most of their lives in service to their country. All three were educated by the French and trained to protect their homeland and the freedom and democracy for which it stood.

When the war first started, my Dad was in a Catholic Seminary studying to be a priest. He dropped out of the seminary and enrolled in the Vietnamese Armed Forces Academy in Đà Lạt, an elite officer school established by the French and supported by the Americans. It was located in a beautiful resort town high in the mountains of Central Vietnam. There he graduated at the top of his officer class and was selected to be in the South Vietnamese top gun special forces and paratroopers.

He quickly rose through the ranks and was appointed mayor of Long Thành District. After serving there for four years, and for doing such a good job, he was promoted to mayor of an even larger and more important district called Quãng Xuyên just across the Saigon River, outside of the Capitol City. My Dad served eight years, and it was there at the mayor's residence that my little sister Huyên (Ti') was born.

From left to right: Mom, Hưng, Huyền, Tí, Hùng, Vui, Lêvi

Under his leadership, the people of the district did well and prospered in relative peace. The people of Quãng Xuyên loved him while he was their leader, and even after he got promoted and moved on they remembered him well. The successful businessmen and women of

Quãng Xuyên often visited my parents during important holidays bringing gifts and souvenirs.

During the turbulent days of April 1975, My Dad, Cậu Năm and Dượng Bảy formulated a plan to move the families to Quãng Xuyên to avoid the communists' bombardment, but my Mom was dead set against it.

"Rồi mình sẽ đi đâu?" she asked. Then where would we go?

She wanted to stay and hunker down, the general mindset at the time. So we stayed at our residence in Trần Hưng Đạo, double locking the doors and windows, eating dehydrated rice and American MREs (meals ready to eat) that Cậu Năm had stockpiled.

On Tuesday, April 29, the situation in Saigon deteriorated and the Americans accelerated the evacuation of their personnel and families. When the American van pulled up to their hideouts, people had to decide at a moment's notice whether to stay or to go. Those that could not make up their minds were usually left behind to fend for themselves.

Tuesday, April 29, 1975 at the US Embassy in Saigon

After days of heavy bombardment, Tân Sơn Nhất Airport outside of Saigon was captured by the communists. In the sky, a steady stream of helicopters came and went from the rooftop of the US Embassy in downtown Saigon, where they tried to evacuate hundreds of people that had gathered inside the compound and on the other side of the walled fence. On the streets, soldiers and civilians continued to build more and larger makeshift barricades to block the communist tanks from entering the city. Artillery shells rained down steadily, and before long small arms fire could be heard throughout the city.

Photo © Dirck Halstead

Tuesday, April 29, 1975 at the US Embassy in Saigon

From the terrace of our four-storied home, we witnessed Saigon's destruction firsthand. Many soldiers, angered by the the Americans' betrayal, fired their handguns and semi-automatic rifles at the helicopters flying high above. Then, venting their frustration, they turned their guns and fired randomly at tall buildings. No helicopters were hit, but it was certainly frightening for the people onboard and for those desperate to get on them. Our parents made us go downstairs, fearing we might get shot, but the boys, including my brothers, cousins and I, kept sneaking up there to see the action. It was scary and exciting at the same time.

Explosions were becoming more frequent and closer to our home, and all the prayers that we had said did not slow them down or make them go away. And at noon, against my Mom's and Dì Bảy's wishes, my Dad, Cậu Năm and Dượng Bảy set out to survey the city. They hoped to find a safe passage to get us out of town.

When they did not come home at one o'clock as promised, my Mom, Dì Bảy (my Mom's younger sister and the wife of Dượng Bảy), and Mợ Năm (the wife of my Mom's older brother Cậu Năm) became really worried. When the clock struck two, we started to say the rosary and prayers for the three men. The hour of three came and went as we continued to say more prayers and rosaries.

Finally, around five o'clock that evening, my Dad, Cậu Năm and Dượng Bảy drove up in a large flatbed white Ford truck. Behind the front seats were an assortment of handguns, grenades and M-16 semi-automatic rifles. Their faces were ashen, and their wide eyes spoke of horror they did not dare verbalize. There was no time for a happy reunion, as they barked orders for us to finish packing so we could get out as quickly as possible.

Thanks to Cậu Năm and Dượng Bảy's experience and advanced preparation, each of us, and there were more than twenty of us kids under twenty-years-old among the three families, was well packed. In our pillowcases, there were two sets of clothing, two MRE rations, two dehydrated rice packages, and perhaps one little toy or some candies. The older kids helped carry the families' important papers and assorted care packages for the babies.

While I was not old enough to be classified as a "big kid," Dad assigned me to carry Huy-Hoàng's baggage and to keep my eyes on him at all times. My older brother Hưng was to carry my baby sister Hà's; my oldest brother Hùng was to carry my younger sister Huyền's; and my older sister Lêvi was to take care of my other younger sister Huyên, if necessary. Everything was planned, military style.

Our cousins from Nha Trang were much more prepared, as they

had been through this before during their evacuation. They had been staying at our home and had taught us how to pack and get ready. They each prepared similar pillowcases and labeled theirs with a red felt tip pen. They were quick to follow orders and seemed more excited than we were about leaving.

Then in the final minutes prior to boarding the truck, my Mom had a change of plan. She wanted my oldest brother Hùng, who was nineteen at the time, to stay behind and watch the house. This caused a serious fight between my parents.

My Mom's years of hard work in building wealth for our family, while my Dad was out fighting for the country, was too much for her to leave behind. She felt that if there was any hope we could return home that my brother would keep the house intact for us. My Dad insisted that there would be no return, that we would either die together or make it out of the country together. They started this argument weeks earlier, but it had never been resolved. Now it was time for a decision.

As we sat crammed together in the bed of the pickup watching, Mom and Dad argued with fervent passion. Both were crying. The decision to leave their oldest son behind might be his death sentence. Yet if the communists took over the city, we would never be able to come back to our house unless we could prove that we lived there all along. Cậu Năm and Dì Bảy pleaded with my Mom to let Hùng go with us.

My Dad, afraid of losing his oldest child, kept asking Hùng, *"Con dám ở lại giữ nhà một mình không?"* Can you handle staying and watching the home by yourself?

Scared but trying to appear fearless, my teenage brother Hùng said *Yes*.

My Mom gave him a sack of cash and held onto him for a long time. She was weeping and praying that she had done the right thing. My Dad gave him a handgun and a semi-automatic rifle. Then he gave Hùng instructions on how to get out of the country in case things got worse or if he did not hear from my Dad within the next couple days.

As he watched the loaded Ford truck speed away, my brother Hùng stood solemnly at the front entrance. Tearfully, we kids waved good-bye in silence.

Cậu Năm drove through the streets of Saigon, while my Dad and Dượng Bảy sat by the windows pointing their M-16s outward at the streets, as if to say *"Don't mess with us."* The streets were full of trash and abandoned automobiles, trucks and military uniforms. The barricades that were set up to stop the communist tanks from entering the city now made it difficult for our truck to navigate to the Saigon River, but somehow we managed to drive around the obstacles or over them.

We drove by the large statue of South Vietnamese soldiers near the National Opera House and saw several dead bodies of South Vietnamese officers that had committed suicide there. Families and loved ones gathered around the bodies weeping; the same scenes were repeated throughout the city. We got near Bến Tàu (Port of Saigon) and the place was a scene of mass hysteria, with people swarming, pushing and shoving each other, trampling anybody in their way to get onto any ship or small boat that would take them out to sea. Large families like ours, with so many young children, would not have a chance getting on the same boat together.

Cậu Năm made a quick turn from the main port and started to look for small ferries or fishing boats. When he and his family had fled Nha Trang, they had commandeered a boat and headed out to sea toward Saigon just minutes before the communists took over Nha Trang. This experience prepared him for what we had to do now.

He soon found several small fishing boats farther down the river. My Dad, Cậu Năm and Dượng Bảy negotiated with the fishermen and paid them with stacks of cash for two boats to take us to Quảng Xuyên.

It started to rain as we boarded the tiny fishing boats and it seemed as though God was weeping for the poor Vietnamese leaving their homes. Mom, Dì Bảy and Mợ Năm cried as the fishing boats pushed out into the brown water of the Saigon River and scores of boats and ships of all sizes queued up and headed out to sea. Each vessel was grossly overloaded with people and there was barely room for anybody to sit down.

Thirty minutes later, we arrived at a small fishing village in Quảng Xuyên. The village leaders were happy to see my Dad alive, and they welcomed us with hospitality typical of Southern Vietnamese people. They quickly cleaned up the village conference hall, which was an open slab of concrete with a corrugated metal roof, and brought us food and drink. After dinner, while the men sat down with the village leaders to discuss what was going on, we kids went down to the riverside and watched the convoy of boats and ships leaving the Port of Saigon.

From afar, we heard gunfire and explosions and saw smoke rising from burning buildings in the city. While we watched from the river bank late into the night, the convoy of vessels continued nonstop with their lights turned off and engines running slow and quiet to not attract attention. People were heading silently into the night, uncertain of their destination, unsure of a future. Against the dark sky, we could see clearly the red and yellow flames billowing from many buildings in Saigon. And as the night progressed towards morning and more and more buildings were consumed by flames, we prayed that my brother Hùng was alright.

Saigon River in the dark

That night, we slept on the concrete floor away from home, while my Dad, Cậu Năm and Dượng Bảy stood watch holding their rifles.

In the early hours of Wednesday, April 30, we were awakened by the sounds of rapid gunfire and blasts coming from across the river. As more smoke columns appeared, it seemed as though violent fighting had broken out all over the city. On the river, there were fewer boats now and the boats were smaller with more people in them.

The people of Quảng Xuyên gave us boiled eggs and rice cakes for breakfast, and the village leader rolled out a small black and white TV so we could watch the news.

At 10 o'clock that morning, the head of South Vietnam's interim government, Dương Văn Minh, appeared and surrendered to Communist North Vietnam. The Vietnam War was now over and the Country of Vietnam was unified under Communist rule.

For my Dad and Dượng Bảy, it was a death sentence. Not only were their military careers over, but also they had now become major liabilities to their beloved families and would be hunted down and killed without mercy by the victors. South Vietnam, which my Dad had risked his life time after time, was no more. The wounds of war that scarred his body and nearly killed him so many times had been in vain.

Việt Cộng entered Independence Hall on April 30, 1975

He stood somberly, staring at the television screen, not hearing or seeing anything. My Mom covered her mouth in horror and cried again. Next to them, also crying, Dượng Bảy hugged Dì Bảy tightly. And nearby, Cậu Năm was holding onto Mợ Năm's hands, shaking his head in disbelief.

After a long silence, my Dad turned to the leader of the village, who was visibly shaken, and spoke to him quietly; the man went off to prepare a small wooden fishing boat for us. The boat was about the size of an oversized American bass boat, perhaps eight feet by twenty feet. There were thirty of us in the three extended families, and Dượng Bảy picked up sixteen more people from his side of the family at the last minute, so forty-six of us boarded a boat that was barely seaworthy. Even so, we cast off and headed down the Saigon River.

Vietnamese River Boat

The boat sat so low in the water that, sitting at the edge with Huy-Hoàng on my lap; we were able to touch the brown river water. The small outboard motor struggled to move us forward against the uncooperative current. The sky was gray with low clouds that day. There was little wind, and the smell of the muddy river combined with the fishy odor of the boat was clearly noticeable. We must have been one of the last small boats to leave, as there were hardly any other boats around us, unlike the convoy that we had seen the night before.

The river opened up wider as we made our way downriver, and the waves increased in size and frequency. My Dad and Dượng Bảy got to the front of the boat and stared out at the large river with anxious looks on their faces. Every time a wave hit, the brown brackish water spilled into the boat. The rain started up again, and in no time we were drenched. It was difficult to tell if it was the rain or the waves that caused the water to rise inside the overloaded boat. My Mom took our baby sister Hà into the covered part of the boat to keep her dry.

The fishing boat was typical of the wooden riverboats that provided a livelihood for fishermen and their families along the rivers of South Vietnam. The boat was slightly larger than one hundred square feet and was designed to house no more than ten people. Most of the inside surface of the boat was bare, and sometimes people put a modest cover on the rear of the boat to protect its small engine. The front of the boat was built to be higher than that of the rear, and a platform was usually installed at the front as a work surface. Fishermen used these boats to creep along the banks of the river to catch shrimp and small fish.

The boat was clearly not designed to hold forty-six people, and we were so close to the water that there was a real danger of tipping over or being swamped. There was not enough space for us to sit, so except for the ones that could sit on the edge of the boat, everyone else had to stand and hold tightly to one another. As we moved farther downriver, the waves got larger and, since most of us were standing, tossed us around like rag dolls. The water rose quickly inside the boat and the fisherman running the motor got really scared. He had never gone this far down the river before with such a heavy load.

He protested to my Dad, *"Dạ thưa Trung Tá, tàu này đi không nổi nữa dâu. Xin Trung Tá cho em quay về, chớ không thì chắt sẽ chết hết, Trung Tá ơi."* Lieutenant Colonel, this boat just cannot take it anymore. Please let us go back, or else I think we will all die here soon.

My Dad disagreed. *"Chú cứ tiếp tục mà đi. Không có được quay về đâu hết, nghe chưa,"* he said, grasping the butt of the handgun at his side. Just keep going. We are not turning around, you hear?

On the way to South China Sea

The fisherman, having to choose between drowning and a bullet, quietly responded, *"Thế là xong rồi. Thế là xong rồi."* Oh, no. This is it. This is it.

But we kept moving forward. It was amazing to see how a man with a gun could get what he wanted.

A little past noon, while we were busy bailing water from the boat, Cậu Năm noticed another boat fast approaching from behind. As it came closer, we saw that it was a larger steel utility boat, one abandoned by the American Forces. While it was larger, about fifteen by forty feet, it was crammed with more than two hundred and fifty people, but it handled the waves far better than the one we were on.

We motioned frantically for them to stop, but as we tried to get closer, the boat steered away from us, not even slowing down

Then my Dad made a daring move. He ordered the fisherman to cut across the path of the larger boat. Reluctantly, the fisherman obeyed as I choked back a scream.

The larger boat was unable to stop and hit us hard, right where I was sitting and holding Huy Hoàng. It lifted our side of the boat up high and slammed it down brutally into the brown water, pushing us out of its way. Water poured in over the gunnels from all directions. Everyone on our boat yelled to the people on the utility vessel to stop and save us.

On board the larger boat, a Catholic priest pleaded with the captain to stop. Other people screamed in horror and demanded he pick us up from our sinking fishing boat before we drowned. Like a miracle, the bigger boat slowed down to let us get closer.

Dad ordered the fisherman to dock with the larger boat and then told me to get Huy-Hoàng onto the utility vessel as soon as the two touched. He turned around and ordered everyone to prepare to board as quickly as possible.

Almost completely filled with water, our sluggish boat struggled fiercely against the wake of the larger one, and managed to get close to the right side of the other boat. As soon as the two boats touched, I threw Huy-Hoàng as hard as I could into the arms of people on the other boat. Then they reached out and pulled each one of us onto their deck.

My Mom sitting in the back of the fishing boat holding onto Hà was paralyzed with fear and could not move. My Dad and Dượng Bảy grabbed her and Hà and pushed them onto the larger boat. Dượng Bảy and my Dad were the last ones to get onboard. In the moment of adversity, the calmness and deliberate actions of Dượng Bảy and my Dad were a true life lesson and it etched permanently in my memory.

In the confusion, we kids were scattered all around the deck. Frantically, Dì Bảy, Mợ Năm and Mom looked around trying to find us all. When no one could find Huy-Hoàng, my Mom panicked.

"Huy-Hoàng đâu? Huy-Hoàng đâu?" she wailed loudly in

desperation, holding Hà tightly. Where's Huy-Hoang? Where's Huy-Hoang?

My Dad looked at me and shouted the same anxious question. I told them I had thrown Huy-Hoàng aboard. But thinking that I had thrown Huy-Hoàng into the river, my Mom cried out like an injured animal, keening and screaming Huy-Hoàng's name repeatedly into the murky water.

Agonizing minutes passed before a stranger from the other side of the boat brought a crying Huy-Hoàng to us. *"Con của cô phải không?"* she said. This is your son, right?

My Mom's eyes lit up and she grabbed Huy-Hoàng, pulled him to her side and embraced him. My Dad smiled at me as my legs shook and I sunk to my knees. We all huddled against each other, so happy that we had made it onto the big boat.

As Dad went to thank the priest, my Mom, Dì Bảy and Mợ Năm tossed sacks filled with Vietnamese currency down to the fisherman, whose boat was now lighter and more manageable. The joyous fisherman waved good-bye and sped back up river toward Quảng Xuyên.

Our happiness was short-lived, however, as the vessel suddenly sputtered and stalled, unable to move toward the open sea. Luckily, Dượng Bảy knew something about engines and hurried to the engine compartment to work on it with the other men.

Thirty minutes later, the engine started again and the boat moved forward steadily. Dượng Bảy, completely stained with black engine oil, appeared on deck and smiled proudly, as my Dad and Cậu Năm shook his hands and patted him on the back. He was the hero of our new vessel, and the passengers who previously were not that happy to see us were now glad to have us and especially Dượng Bảy on board.

On the way out to sea, we saw several broken-down boats littering the river. Some were full of people, but we could not risk stopping the fragile engine to pick them up, so we kept on going. As we left

Saigon River and approached the open sea, the sun set on the horizon and the cold winds blew over the water. Our vessel struggled against the waves, but managed to keep moving away from the land of the newly united Vietnam.

Our boat was so crammed that my sister Lêvi and I were allotted only a little space to sleep on, an elevated square near the boat's flag pole. Beside us was a young couple in their early twenties. The young man, dressed in a South Vietnamese officer's uniform, had taken poison in a suicide attempt and now was fighting to stay alive. His breathing was shallow and his young bride was holding onto him, sobbing and praying all night long. I joined her and silently said my prayers for him, for her, for my family, my extended family and everyone else on the boat. I prayed for the country I had just left behind, and trusted God for what was to come. Then I said a special prayer for my older brother Hùng who was still in Saigon.

I glanced toward the stern of the boat and caught my Dad's lips moving quietly as he stood at the edge of the boat praying and looking back at the country he loves. Later he told me that even though he had lived through many fierce battles, where life and death were hanging by a thread and that faith was the only factor for his survival, he had never totally surrendered his entire family into the Hands of God as he had that day on the Saigon River.

My Dad, the fearless peaceful warrior, had become the anchor of faith; and his battle experience had trained him to face adversity with composure and deliberation. May God bless him with courage to face the calamity of the days to come.

That night, the sea was wonderfully calm, with millions of stars blinking above. There were no more sounds of gunfire, no explosions, only the rhythmic magic of waves rocking the vessel's hull, and I quickly fell asleep on my sister's shoulder.

Tomorrow, we would wake up as refugees, a people without a country.

CHAPTER FOUR

Refugees

If you pass through raging waters
In the sea, you shall not drown.

You shall speak your words in foreign lands,
And all will understand,
You shall see the Face of God and live.

Be not afraid,
I go before you always,
Come follow Me,
And I shall give you rest.
-- Old Catholic Hymn

Thursday May 1, 1975, was a magnificent day at sea. The water was as calm and unruffled as a sheet of glass, and the gentle north breeze cooled the air and made us feel comfortable.

My sister Lêvi woke me early to watch the sunrise, and see its rays bounce and dance as they hit the water. The gentle rolling waves of clear blue water extended all the way to the horizon. The sky was bright and the red sun was huge and dazzling.

We were in the middle of the South China Sea in the Pacific Ocean with no land in sight, alone with the calming hum from the engine compartment. My Mom waved the two of us to the rear of the boat where the rest of the family gathered around her. It felt good to see them safe and in high spirits, and equally good to see that the young soldier had survived the night. His allotted space showed signs that he had vomited, and he was now able to sit up. By his side, his young wife sat with her head on his shoulder and her arms wrapped around him. Alive with peace and love.

When Lêvi and I sat down, we saw that Huy Hoàng was already up and amusing himself. He and Trâm, Dì Bảy's little girl, were playing with the little green cans of MREs. Their laughter cheered everyone around us. Mom handed us crackers and jam from the MRE packages, and they tasted so good, you would have thought they were from an Emperor's breakfast. People watched enviously, so my Mom told us not to make a big fuss about it. She mixed some milk and fed Hà. Hà was content in her arms, and I wondered who was happier.

My Dad was the highest ranking officer on the boat, so he summoned the other men to the back of the boat for a conference to decide what we should do next. After a short while, Dad came back and made an announcement that we were heading to Đảo Côn Sơn (Con Son Island), which was about sixty miles southeast of mainland Vietnam. They'd heard that the US Navy's Seventh Fleet was picking up refugees there. Everyone felt this was a good course of action and were hopeful that the Americans would save us.

The boat headed south and picked up speed, and Lêvi and I went back to our designated area. I stopped briefly and gave the soldier and his wife some of my crackers and jam that I'd kept in my pocket for later. The girl looked up at me, tired but grateful, nodded quietly and offered a polite smile.

Around noon, we could see Đảo Côn Sơn in the distance. As we got closer, we saw many small boats and large ships lined up around the islands. Đảo Côn Sơn was composed of a series of small islands with one large main island in the center. The French had built a prison on the main isle and that was where they had kept political prisoners and hardcore criminals. Later the South Vietnamese Regime filled the prison and assumed control of the islands. The islands were heavily wooded and beautiful, seeming to stand majestically in the middle of the ocean with no sandy beaches but many rocky cliffs. In a way, they looked like the cliffs of Vịnh Hà Long in North Vietnam. When we saw the islands, everyone was happy and excited. It was the first time that I saw my Mom, Dì Bảy and Mợ Năm smile in days.

About five miles out, a US Navy attack boat intercepted us and demanded that we stop. Dượng Bảy told Cậu Năm, who was the only one on our boat that could speak English, to yell back to the Americans that our boat would not start again if we cut the engine. He shouted out our message, but the soldiers insisted that we stop immediately, their machine guns pointing at the people on our smaller vessel.

My Dad ordered the captain to stop and the US boat circled us and told Cậu Năm we should throw our weapons into the sea. I did not know where all the handguns, grenades, and semi-automatic rifles came from, but they seemed to appear out of nowhere and were tossed into the water. Satisfied, the Americans said we could join the boats and ships near the islands.

When Cậu Năm translated the encouraging words, everyone on our boat was glad, but, just as Dượng Bảy had predicted, our engine would not restart. Our hearts sank, but fortunately, sailors on the US attack boat threw us a large rope as a tow and hauled us toward the islands.

As we neared the convoy, my Dad spotted a Vietnamese Naval ship numbered "07" and signaled Cậu Năm to ask the US boat to pull us toward the ship. And they did. My Dad turned to my Mom and told her that the Vietnamese Naval Destroyer Number 07 was under the command of one of our relatives named Dượng Hưng, and that we would be better off with him. Mom was thankful that we had a relative within the convoy, and told Dad to go ahead. Dad, the highly decorated military commander, was the boss, but my Mom was the ultimate authority in family matters.

As we pulled alongside his ship, Dượng Hưng was happy to see my Dad. He ordered his shipmates to lower a large net and they helped us get aboard. He yelled down and asked, *"Vợ tôi có đi được với Anh không?"* Did my wife come out with you?

My Dad shook his head sadly and answered no. And Dượng Hưng

became distraught. He turned and looked away for a moment, and when he looked back, there were tears in his eyes.

Dượng Hưng and my Dad were more than just cousins growing up in Nha Trang. They were soccer buddies since they were little. And they were patriots: Dượng Hưng became a cadet at the Vietnamese Naval Academy while my Dad went to the Officer Academy. They had kept in touch throughout their careers. Like my Dad, Dượng Hưng did quite well and was commissioned to command his own ship, a privilege reserved for high ranking naval officers of the South Vietnamese Navy.

His family moved from Nha Trang and resided in Vũng Tàu, a touristy beach town 50 miles outside of Saigon. During the fall of Saigon, Dượng Hưng's wife (Mợ Hưng) was more than eight months pregnant; they also had three other small children. Early on, my Mom and Dad had asked her to join us if we were to leave Vietnam, but Mợ Hưng declined. She felt safer staying for the sake of the baby she was carrying and her young children.

Once we boarded Dượng Hưng's ship, my Mom and Dad informed Dượng Hưng of his wife's decision. And the man broke down. He was in so much pain missing his wife and children, and the new baby that he might never know, that he sobbed loudly in front of all of us.

Dượng Hưng had been away from his family for months shuttling soldiers and supplies to and from the front lines, and he only had limited communication with his family. When President Nguyễn Văn Thiệu resigned, his admiral ordered all South Vietnamese navy ships to station at Côn Sơn and not to return to port. The collapse of Saigon happened so quickly that he could not get word to his wife and family to join him.

So he cried. My Mom and Dad tried their best to comfort him, but to no avail. Dượng Hưng was so upset that he just wanted to go home to his pregnant wife and his children. My Dad told him about the situation in Saigon and the dangers awaiting a high ranking officer like him in the mainland. My Dad asked him to calm down before making any hasty decisions. He listened to my Dad and went to his captain's room to cry.

Meanwhile all of us had boarded Dương Hưng's ship without incident. His shipmates treated us with utmost respect. Knowing that we were family, they took great care to feed us and gave Mom and Dad an air conditioned room reserved for visiting VIPs while other people were sent to the lower decks.

Dương Hưng's ship was one of only a handful of destroyers run by the South Vietnamese Navy. The Americans built it and gave it to them, and it was enormous with at least three or four decks. The top deck was equipped with heavy weaponry and electronic control equipment. Below, the decks were reserved for transporting personnel, supplies and weapons. Dương Hưng's ship was full of naval personnel, among them more than 100 South Vietnamese Marines, all sorts of weapons and supplies.

After settling in her room, my Mom sent my Dad to check on Dương Hưng. And it was a good thing that he did. My Dad found Dương Hưng in his room with a handgun to his head.

My Dad pleaded with him to stop and to choose life. Dương Hưng listened to his good friend, but his heart was broken. When he saw us kids running around, it reminded him of his own family and he could not hold back his tears.

Later that afternoon, the US Seventh Fleet ordered the convoy to head for the Philippines. When word came that we were about to depart, many of Dương Hưng's soldiers and navy men, who had not seen their families for a long time, asked Dương Hưng to let them use the lifeboats to go back to the mainland. Knowing the dangers awaiting them, Dương Hưng tried to convince them not to go, but in the end, more than several dozen men said they wanted to leave and Dương Hưng ordered the lifeboats lowered.

It was very sad to see grown men and soldiers, strip off their uniforms and don civilian clothing. They were willing to risk their lives for the love of their families to return to a country that no longer welcomed them.

As the fleet set sail for the Philipines, Dượng Hưng tried to jump into a lifeboat to go home with them, and my Dad, Dượng Bảy and Cậu Năm grabbed him and held him back. All four of them were in tears. So were many of us.

It took three days at sea for our convoy to go from Đảo Côn Sơn, Vietnam, to Subic Bay in the Philippines. During that trip, Dượng Hưng allowed us kids to roam the huge ship freely, except for the weaponry and soldiers' decks. From the captain's control room, we could see out for miles. There must have been more than forty US naval ships and perhaps hundreds of Vietnamese naval ships, civilian vessels and other boats in the convoy. Due to its defense capabilities, Dượng Hưng's ship was situated near the head of the convoy, and that gave us an amazing view of the never-ending ocean in front of us, as well as the massive entourage behind our ship.

After the sun rose, the deck of the ship became scorching hot, and it could easily burn our feet walking on it. Dượng Hưng ordered his men to throw heavy Army tarps over the entire deck so we could run around, and it was wonderful. We chased each other and then settled down in the shade under the lifeboats. At lunch, the ship's cooks prepared hot meals of noodles, rice and meatballs, and we ate and talked and laughed like we were on an expensive cruise around the world. And then when evening came, the ocean wind cooled our skins and made being alive a joy. Dinner time was much the same, enjoying the breeze while eating meals of hot meats and rice and watching the sunset. Then at night, lights from other ships in the convoy lit up the water just like a moving city.

I would lie back on the deck under the starlit sky, and wonder about the friends I had left behind. As a good student and a team leader, I always got selected by the priests to calculate the scores and report cards for the class; so I remembered all the names of my classmates, and how each was ranked within the order of the class. I often thought about how they must have felt when my Mom took me out of school. I was certain that, day-by-day, more and more students would be taken out of class, and I wondered who would be left behind and how scared they would be. Then I thought about the priests and the teachers and if they would abandon their students to help their own families escape.

I missed the routine of the life of a seminarian, the hours of praying, playing soccer and volleyball, the simple meals, and the long study periods. I said many prayers for my seminarian friends and other people left behind, and often wondered if we would ever meet any of them again.

And then I started to dream about America. I had seen American movies and thought about the land of cowboys, the deserts of the American west, snow-capped mountains, and sheaves of amber grain waving in the wind. I dreamed about apples, chocolate, chewing gum, candies and ice cream. When I fell asleep, I was happy.

We arrived in the Philippines late one afternoon. As we approached from a distance, the islands shimmered in the heat, the water frothed and the mountains disappeared into the sky. We saw Filipino fishermen on their unusual fishing boats on which several wooden poles projected out from both sides and attached to a float or log to stabilize the boat in the water so it didn't capsize.

What a beautiful country. So peaceful. So free of war.

The US Navy ordered us to stop and drop anchor away from port. Vietnamese soldiers had to surrender their weapons, remove their rank insignia, and allow US Navy personnel to take over their ships. It was heartbreaking to see South Vietnamese soldiers and officers lined up on deck and one by one throw their weapons and badges into the ocean. Many of them had tears in their eyes.

The US Navy personnel then lowered the red striped yellow flag of South Vietnam and raised the Stars and Stripes of the United States of America, while playing the US national anthem. I could see many former soldiers and officers with tears running down their faces watching the US flag climb the pole. My Dad, Dượng Bảy, Cậu Năm and Dượng Hưng stood next to each other, wiping away tears, trying hard not to cry out loud.

When it was our turn to dock at port and disembark, it was two o'clock in the morning. The Americans rushed us into a huge hangar flooded with lights, where there were thousands of Vietnamese refugees like us waiting in line to be processed. Some refugees did not have baggage; some came with suitcases, as though they were on vacation. We carried our humble pillow cases and each of our families huddled together tightly in clumps to keep from getting lost.

We waited in line until the early hours of the morning. An American official rubber stamped our hands and then asked every one of us the same question, which we could not understand, but Cậu Năm had instructed us to say *yes*. Then we moved onto the next line, where another official told us to sign a piece of paper we could not read, and gave us several pages of forms to keep. Then we were shunted toward a waiting area, where there must have been another ten thousand or more Vietnamese refugees standing around looking bewildered.

At noon, we were instructed to line up in front of a gigantic super tanker named "Green Forest." The Green Forest was one of the largest crude oil tankers at the time. It had more than six levels and each level was larger than several football fields combined. The crude was hastily washed out, but the oil smell was nauseating.

It took hours to load everyone onto the gargantuan ship. Each family was given a square of five feet by five feet that was outlined by duct tape on the sludgy metal floor. Since our family was large, we were allotted two squares. Cậu Năm and Dượng Bảy's families were nearby, and they too got two squares each. Dượng Hưng was grouped with other single men. We were in the middle level without windows, crammed in with thousands of refugees.

They kept us within our squares for several hours while loading the rest of the people. The smell and the heat made us sick and contributed to our exhaustion. Hà and Huy Hoàng were crying and everyone else was miserable. Mom took out the few MREs remaining in our pillow cases, and gave us something to eat. Other families nearby that were not prepared went hungry.

As there were no bathroom facilities down below, the Americans built makeshift wooden bathrooms all along the outside of the deck hanging fifty feet or so above the water. To go up on deck, we had to climb wooden ladders made out of two by fours. When the ship was moving on the high sea later on, the wind, the vibration and the motion of the waves made using the bathroom a precarious adventure. And for people afraid of heights, it was a terrifying experience.

The Green Forest Super Tanker

The Green Forest departed Subic Bay that evening and the people on board cheered as the tanker sailed out of port. Many raced up the ladders to go on deck for fresh air, others rushed to the opening between levels to catch some air. The Americans passed out food packages composed of crackers and some sort of stew for dinner, and people started to feel better after they ate.

The trip from Subic Bay to the Island of Guam was a long and miserable one. Besides the discomfort of the vessel, the sea was rough. Some days, giant waves of thirty and forty feet thrashed the tanker like a toy boat in a bathtub; and then the strong winds picked up right before it rained. The people that were assigned the spaces under the openings of the tanker had to move when the rain came. The rain water collected on the decks made the floors slippery and dangerous. During those storms, many people got sea sick and were throwing up and groaning and everyone suffered.

On clear days, many of us took turns going up on deck for fresh air only to get wet either from the salt water crashing over the sides of the ship or from the hanging toilets located all around the outside of the ship. For a guy that got motion sickness easily, I was a wreck. Depending on the condition of the sea, I went on deck several times a day to vomit. Surprisingly, my brothers, sisters and cousins held up quite well.

When the Green Forest finally reached Guam, it was a blessing from heaven. As much as we had prayed to get on the ship, now we prayed to get off! It was late in the night, and again, it took many hours to unload the thousand upon thousands of Vietnamese refugees. I didn't know that solid ground could feel so good. Guam was our first landing on US soil, and there were more lines, but this time the Americans also gave us a quick medical checkup. During the processing ordeal, our three families got split up. They loaded us onto Army trucks that were lined up by the hundreds, and drove us to different refugee camps on the island.

The refugee camps, set up hurriedly by American GIs on the far end of the island, were surrounded by chain-link fencing with barbed wire on top. When our truck reached the gates, I wondered if the fence was for our protection, keeping us inside the camp, or was it to keep the American anti-war protesters out.

Once inside, I saw thousands of tents set up directly on the red clay. Inside each tent were a dozen cots, and one single light bulb hung by a wire in the middle. For each row of a dozen tents or so, there was a blue portable toilet at one end. And for each hundred tents in the camp, there was one communal bathroom for men and one for women. American soldiers delivered water on water trucks daily to be used for bathing and drinking.

Each tent was to house at least two families, but for our large family, we got a tent to ourselves. My Mom cried when the American guide showed us our designated tent. As we sat down on the cots and tried to fan ourselves from the oppressive heat, my Dad tried his best to comfort her.

There was one dining hall per camp. The hall was nothing more than a much larger tent where the Americans prepared and served food and where we could sit on benches and eat. Already hundreds of people were lining up to get food.

I asked my Dad to let me go check out the dining hall, then my brother Hưng and I ran out to get in line. After waiting for more than an hour, we each got two slices of white bread, some stew and a scoop of peach cobbler on a paper plate. We rushed "home" and showed my Mom and Dad, and then my sisters, Hưng and I ran back to get in line again.

After lunch, I found a line for baby food and diapers for Hà and Huy Hoàng. I was quite happy with my discovery and did not mind waiting in yet another line. My Mom was pleased that the Americans gave us enough to eat and took care of our younger ones. The lines for dinner started at 3:30 PM, and I was in line again to repeat the same routine that I did for lunch. I hung around different lines most of the day and had quite a good time.

Later that day, I went to the dumpster and found a five gallon bucket. I then went to the water distribution center and filled it to the rim to take back to our tent. My Mom needed the water to bathe Hà and Huy Hoàng. After their baths, they both seemed much happier and more alert. They did look a bit funny in the ill-fitting diapers, as if they had been stuffed into an oversized sack. The single light bulb turned on automatically at 7:00 PM. The cots were uncomfortable, but at least we did not have to sleep on the dirt floor or inhale oil fumes. Exhausted, we all fell asleep by nine. To our surprise, there were no mosquitoes in Guam.

Next morning, my Dad left early to post a message at the Administration Center looking for my older brother Hùng, just in case he had made it out. He then went to find Cậu Năm and Dượng

Bảy and their families. He found Cậu Năm's family first at one of the camps in the far end. Cậu Năm had already made new friends with other Vietnamese families around his tent and when they found out he could speak English quite well, they asked him to help them with translation matters. Cậu Năm was now a celebrity in his own camp. Later Cậu Năm volunteered to work with the American camp administrators to help other refugees.

On the way back to our camp, my Dad found Dì Bảy, Dượng Bảy and their children housed not too far from us. And they claimed to have better food and cleaner bathrooms, because not all of the tents in their camp were occupied yet. My Dad was quite happy that their family was alright.

The sanitary conditions of the Guam camps were at best lacking. The toilets and bathroom facilities were crude and dirty, the dust that was whipped up by the wind swirled into our faces, food, clothes and tent. As a result, my sister Lêvi and I suffered severe eye and nose infections shortly after our arrival. We went to the camp clinic and got antibiotic drops and had to stay away from the rest of the family for a while until our conditions improved. Fortunately, no one else in our family got infected. But while we were sidelined, my brother Hưng had to fetch the water and get diapers for the babies by himself. He was glad when I was well enough to assume my water duties again.

One day, when I was carrying the water bucket back to our tent, an American soldier walked by me and asked, "Heavy?" and made a hand carrying gesture. I was totally confused and all night long I could not figure out what he meant. I knew I did not do anything to offend him, and that I took great care not to spill and waste water, but my English was so poor that I could not understand what the friendly American had tried to say to me. Years of studying French in the seminary did not help me now. In the morning, I asked my Dad, what "heavy" means, and then realized that this strange American land would present many challenges, language being only one of them.

Our family remained at the Guam camps for more than a month.

Cậu Năm and his family were the first of our three families to leave for the mainland due to his ability to speak English. Serving as his camp's volunteer interpreter, Cậu Năm was able to get his family processed after only two weeks and he and his family left Guam for Camp Pendleton in California. Shortly thereafter, Dì Bảy, Dượng Bảy and their children took off for Camp Pendleton as well. We were left behind.

It was bittersweet to see our cousins leaving the camps. While we were happy and excited that they were able to go to the US mainland, we were sad and wondered if we would ever see them again. Cậu Năm and Dì Bảy's families were the sweetest people on earth. Their children were well mannered, a pleasure to be around. The older ones were helpful, while the younger ones were polite and kind, and they all got along with us. They talked with an accent typical of people from Nha Trang; otherwise, they were just like us, a bunch of fun-loving kids growing up in a war-torn country.

My Mom and Dad were particularly downcast when we said good-bye to them. The parents of our extended family had been through so much together in recent months, and had learned to lean on each other for strength and comfort. Together they had protected and delivered their families safely to the land of peace and freedom, even though it cost them their entire life savings and accomplishments. They remained calm during the crisis and worked together to take care of us. My Mom was inconsolable when she said good-bye to her younger sister Dì Bảy, the link to her family from the old country. The two ladies held onto each other for a while before Dì Bảy boarded the Army bus for the airport. My Mom was weeping as she waved farewell.

During our stay in Guam, my brother Hưng taught me how to swim at a beach near the camp. Hưng was two years older than me, and had studied at Tu Viện Sao Biển, a seminary right on the beach in Nha Trang near Dì Bảy's house. He could swim like a fish, and was patient enough to show me how to float in the water. He also took French and English in the seminary, so he spoke some English. Hưng also possessed a much more sociable personality, a dominant trait from my Mom, so he was adapting to the people and languages more quickly than I. So every day I followed my brother to the beach and tried to swim, while he was making friends with the Americans. All of our many cousins had long since left us.

One afternoon, my Dad declared that we were to go to a camp at Eglin Air Force Base in Florida. I had no idea why we were not going to Camp Pendleton so we could be with Cậu Năm, Dượng Bảy and their families, but we quickly packed and got ready to go to the US mainland the next day.

At the airport, I told my Dad there was a vending machine that actually sold beer. Even though he was skeptical, he gave me a quarter and told me to get him a cold one. In minutes, I ran back and gave him his "beer". Excited, he opened it and took a sip. Then with a wide grin, he handed the can back to me. He said it was *root beer*, and I did not know what the word "root" meant. It tasted like *"xá xị"* in Vietnam, not like any alcoholic drink my Dad wanted.

The Americans put us on a civilian Boeing 747 from Guam to Florida with a stopover in Hawaii. The huge plane was much fancier than all the other planes I had been on in Vietnam. The food was excellent and the service was exceptional. The pretty hostess served us dinner of beef stew with mashed potatoes accompanied by a can of cold cola. Our family sat together and the flight attendants were kind and kept bringing food and toys for Huy Hoàng and Hà.

During the flight, my Mom told my Dad to ask the flight attendant for a diaper for Hà. And it was so funny watching my Dad trying to describe to the attendant his request using hand gestures. With a puzzled look on her face, the attendant left and minutes later came back with a box of diapers. I was certain that she had had a good laugh with the other attendants.

During the stopover in Hawaii, we could not leave the holding area, but from the airport, we could see the beautiful beaches lined with palm trees, just like those in Nha Trang.

Soon we would be in America.

DEPARTMENT OF THE ARMY
HEADQUARTERS, 45TH SUPPORT GROUP, GUAM
FPO SAN FRANCISCO 96630

AFVG-ONL-CO

Le Cong Chinh
"Operation New Life"
Orote Point Naval Station
FPO San Francisco 96630

Dear Le Cong Chinh:

On the eve of closing Camp Rainbow at Orote Point, Naval Station, Guam,
I would like to express my personal appreciation to you for your invalu-
able assistance in the smooth accomplishment of essential camp operations.
Your skill in organizing and maintaining control over a section of the camp
that was populated by as many as 2,000 persons was a prime factor in
minimizing the number of administrative difficulties we encountered.
Your many innovative ideas and the organization of your staff enabled you
to distribute tons of donated clothing and other relief supplies. You con-
tinually kept the welfare of the people in mind and as a result of your
actions, the camp was a much better place to stop over on the way to the
United States.

The channel of communication that you opened between the people in the
camp and the military administration, facilitated the timely resolution of
many problems that were encountered.

Again, I want to express my appreciation for your co-operation and effec-
tive assistance in handling the multifaceted details of camp operations. I
would like to take this opportunity to wish you and every member of your
family continued good fortune in the new life you are embarking upon.

Sincerely yours,

JOHN D. O'DONOHUE
COL, TC
Commanding

*Thank-you letter from Colonel John O'Donohue to my Dad for his
volunteering work at Guam Island*

CHAPTER FIVE

America

Over the years, the US Government had spent 141 billion dollars and 58,000 American lives, more than 1,000,000 Vietnamese soldiers on both sides, and as many as 2,000,000 South Vietnamese civilians, but they could not stop the ruthless campaign to unify Vietnam under the communist doctrine.

Meanwhile, economic conditions in the US were getting worse. Americans at home saw an increase in unemployment and growing inflation. President Lyndon B. Johnson declined to run for a second term for his perceived failure in handling the war. President Gerald Ford was elected on an anti-war platform that promised to bring a quick end to the Vietnam War.

In 1973, US Secretary of State Henry Kissinger and North Vietnamese Lê Đức Thọ signed the peace treaty in Paris ending the war. The American people were quick to put the war behind them, but the North Vietnamese had a different idea. Two years later, when the Americans least expected it, the communist North Vietnamese overran the borders and captured Saigon, the capitol of South Vietnam.

To be sure, this marked the North's victory in the war; however, the Americans did not completely lose. The US was successful in containing communism long enough to build democracies throughout Southeast Asia from Thailand, to Malaysia, Indonesia, the Philippines and Singapore.

However, with the fall of Saigon, the Americans had a huge humanitarian crisis on their hands. They had to evacuate their personnel, support staff, and Vietnamese loyal to its cause.

The number of Vietnamese refugees seeking political asylum far exceeded the initial estimate of 125,000 by the US Government. Within days after Saigon's collapse, as many as 200,000 refugees were trying to flee Vietnam, and more were on the way. The government hurriedly prepared processing centers in the Philippines, Wake Island and Guam (as my family found out firsthand); and soon realized there were simply too many refugees for those small centers to cope with.

Determined to avoid the mistakes made during the Cuban crisis in the 1960s when the flood of Cuban refugees inundated South Florida, bringing massive unemployment and creating a tremendous drain on local social services, the government set up three major refugee centers spread out across the mainland US: Camp Pendleton in Southern California, Fort Chaffee in Arkansas, and Eglin Air Force Base in Florida. They also readied a small, lesser known facility in Indiantown Gap, Pennsylvania.

Cậu Năm and his family left Guam on a Wednesday night in a military C130 transport plane. During the flight, they were told they were heading to Pennsylvania, instead of Southern California that they had signed up for while in Guam. With no choice, Cậu Năm and his family accepted it as fate. The plane made a brief fuel stop in Hawaii and continued its long flight to Pennsylvania. The refugee camp at Indiantown Gap was an old military barracks left over from World War II, but it was well maintained. Most of the refugees who came to this camp were either former high-ranking South Vietnamese military officers or government officials and their families.

Within a week of their arrival, the Catholic Christian Brothers (Lasan) in Pennsylvania discovered that Dzuy, Cậu Năm's oldest son, was a Christian Brother in Vietnam, and they sponsored Dzuy out of the camp. Meanwhile the Christian Brothers continued to help Cậu Năm and his family to find a sponsor for such a large family. Three weeks later, the Christian Brothers Headquarters took Cậu Năm and his family from the camp and moved them into their seminary near St. Louis. They stayed with the Brothers for a month, and finally were sponsored by a Catholic Parish in St. Louis. The people of the parish helped Cậu Năm find a temporary home, a job and schooling for his children.

By early August 1975, Cậu Năm and his family were able to move into their own home in St. Louis. The parish that sponsored Cậu Năm and his family helped with the down payment for the house. Cậu Năm, Mợ Năm and their family got jobs and eventually paid off the house. St. Louis then became Cậu Năm's first and only home in America.

...

Dượng Bảy wanted to go to Eglin AFB in Florida, where it would be warm for his family, especially for his youngest daughter Susie, who was just several months old at the time. The Americans in charge of processing refugees recommended that Dượng Bảy go elsewhere, because his brother had already been selected to go to Eglin AFB, and they did not want too many relatives in one camp. They were afraid of a mass settlement of Vietnamese in one local community. They asked Dượng Bảy to consider going to Indiantown Gap, so he did.

Dượng Bảy and his family stayed in the Pennsylvania camp for two months. No one wanted to sponsor a family of nine with young children all under eighteen. One day, Dượng Bảy met a Catholic nun who told him about a parish in Cincinnati, Ohio, that might be willing to help. With her recommendation, Dượng Bảy reached out to the parish and was successful in convincing them to sponsor his family.

On August 15, 1975, Dượng Bảy and his family arrived at their new home in Cincinnati, sponsored by the Catholic Parishes of Lady of Lourdes and St. Lawrence. The parishioners got him a job doing general maintenance, and helped his children find schools. Dượng Bảy worked hard, made sacrifices for his children and paid off his house quickly. Dượng Bảy and Dì Bảy still live there to this day.

...

For my immediate family, the transition to American life was not as smooth. The Boeing 747 touched down at Panama City International Airport early in the morning, and already there were several Army buses lined up to take us to the refugee camp at Eglin Air Force Base about thirty miles west of the airport. As we got off the plane, we could see protesters with signs in English that said, "GO HOME." And they screamed at us from behind the airport fence.

It was both confusing and amusing to witness the conflicting attitudes of the American people at the moment that we had arrived. On one hand, I was grateful for the Americans for helping to save us from the tyranny of the Communist Regime. On the other hand, I was amused by the inability of the American people to cope with their overwhelming charitable act. Later I came to appreciate the irony of American freedom and individualism. What they said was not always what they meant and when they said *welcome*, sometimes what they really meant was *go away*.

We were rushed aboard the waiting buses, and immediately they headed for the camp. On the road, we could see that Florida was beautiful in June. The weather was pleasant, not as hot as Guam or Vietnam. And the pine trees along the road were green and stately. We rode by small shopping strips along the way and marveled at the wealth and cleanliness of small town USA. The roads were smooth and free of potholes, and it seemed that everyone had a car. There were no mopeds, no cyclos (a Vietnamese three-wheeled passenger carrying bike), no noisy honking horns while people sat in traffic. Everything seemed to run in order and in perfect harmony. Farther out, houses along the road were pretty with red brick walls and lush landscaping, and so far apart, and there was a sense of peace and calmness about them.

There were more protesters with signs at the camp gates. While not many of us could read English then, by the looks on the faces of the protesters, we suspected those signs said something offensive. The camp was surrounded by a chain-link fence with barbed wire on top, and in light of the angry faces that greeted us at the gate, we were grateful for the security measure.

The camp was arranged with tents similar to those in Guam, but instead of having the tents pitched directly on the dirt, these tents sat on raised wooden platforms. Later I came to learn that the platforms would save us from the monsoon-like rains that flooded these low lying areas. The tall pine trees gave us shade and kept us cool during the heat of the day; and when the winds blew through the trees, their whistling sounds surprised and entertained us, as there were no pine trees in South Vietnam, except in the Central Highlands.

My Mom was pleased now that we had arrived in the US. She knew that we would be okay very soon. My Dad's life had been spared, and perhaps her children would have a better future in this new land. But she worried about my brother Hùng and pushed us hard to see if we could find him. My Dad went to the administration tents around the camp and posted *missing persons* messages on their bulletin boards. He sent letters to other camps in California, Arkansas and Pennsylvania asking about my brother. All of us kids walked throughout the camp looking for Hùng as well. But he was no where to be found, and Dad did not receive replies to his messages.

We did, however, find some of our family's friends and relatives. My Mom and Dad were happy to have people that they knew around them. My brother Hưng met a girl and fell in love, so I could no longer tag along with him. Instead, I hung out with the people of nearby tents and played volleyball. My sister Lêvi babysat the younger ones and helped my Mom fix up clothes given to us by the US Catholic Charity (USCC). And just as Cậu Năm had done earlier, my Dad volunteered to help the American administrators running the camp and that kept him busy, gave him purpose, and cheered him up as well. At the same time, he worked closely with the US Catholic Charity organization trying to find a sponsor for our large family. But no one wanted to sponsor a big family with a houseful of little kids.

The rules at the time said that no one could leave the camp unless they were sponsored by an American family or organization that could provide financial proof that met the qualifications set by the US Government. These rules made it hard for refugees to be sponsored during the tough economic times, but slowly our Vietnamese refugee friends and neighbors at camp got sponsored and moved out. Day after day, we saw people and families leaving the camp, and wondered if we would ever get a patron. Our insecurity grew worse as the hurricane season came upon us. There were days in late June and July that the winds and rain were so fierce, that we wondered if our tent would hold up or if the camp would be blown away.

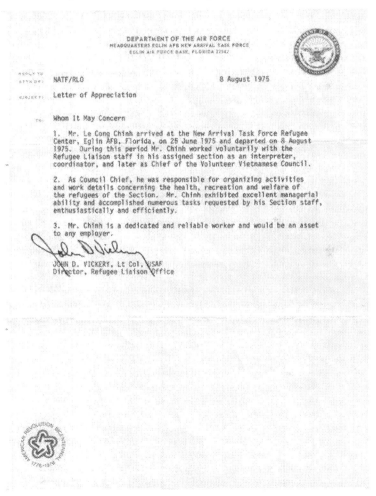

Letter of Appreciation to my Dad from Lt. Col. John Vickery of the US Air Force at Eglin Air Force Base

One day my Dad ran home from his office at the Camp Administration Center with a letter in hand, breathlessly excited.

"Hùng qua được rồi!" he shouted. Hùng had made it! And he gave my Mom the biggest hug. They both danced around the tent, as we kids sat wide-eyed watching.

It seemed that after waiting for us to come home for several days, Hùng followed my Dad's instructions and used the money that my Mom had given him to find a way out of the country. He followed our path to the Port of Saigon and got on one of the boats and left the country by sea, just like us. He ended up at the processing center at Wake Island, and later went to the refugee camp at Fort Chaffee, Arkansas. It was there that he saw my Dad's messages pinned to bulletin boards.

We were so excited, and we sat down to write Hùng to let him know how glad we were that he had made it to the US, and that we could not wait to be reunited. It was wonderful to see my parents so happy after all the setbacks they had encountered.

The following week, my Dad received a letter from Bishop Ernest Unterkoefler of Charleston, South Carolina. Bishop Ernest had received my Dad's letter begging him to sponsor us out of the refugee camp, and he agreed to do so. He and the people of St. John's Parish in North Charleston fixed up a small wooden framed house located at 147 St. John's Avenue with fresh paint and new plumbing. A full work crew headed by Mr. Joseph P. Griffith spent several days getting the house ready and Mr. Wolff of Harverty Furniture Co. donated bedroom furniture. Food and clothing came from the people of parishes all over Charleston. And the house was waiting for us.

My Mom and Dad were overwhelmed with joy. Next stop: Charleston, South Carolina.

July 12, 1975

Dear Sir

I am a VN Refugee and understand from USCC (U.S. Catholic Church) that South Carolina will accepte 10 VN Refugees families. My family is one of these 10 families. I write to you with the great confidence you will help me and my family to be located in a parish in the city of Charby, and help me to get a job so we can have a good life.

About my family, I attended Seminary 7 years (1943-1950), I enlisted 1951 in the VN Army and I am an officier. I had 24 years in army and my rank was Lieutenant Colonel. I speak English and French.

My family contains 9 peoples (my wife, 4 daughters and 3 sons). The oldest daughter is 19 years old and attended 1st year university. One boy 16 years

old has 3 years in Seminary and last
year he was in classe 11 in Saigon.
One boy is 14 years old and also has
3 years in Redemptorist Covent. Both
boys hope to have opportunity to
continue their education.
I send to you the pictures of
every one of my family and one
catholic family certificate from our
catholic parish in V.N.
I hope you will answer my
letter as soon as possible or you
will send some body as sponsor to
come to Eglin AFB to receive my
family to move to your location.
Thank you for your concern
Sincerely

My Dad's letter to Bishop Ernest Unterkoefler

THE DIOCESE OF CHARLESTON

119 BROAD STREET
CHARLESTON, SOUTH CAROLINA 29401

July 18, 1975

OFFICE OF THE BISHOP

Dear Mr. Chinh:

You were most kind to write to me on July 12, 1975, concerning
your wishes to come to South Carolina. I am very interested
in your application and am now in contact with the Very Reverend
Joseph A. Wahl, the Chairman of our committee on Vietnamese
refugees.

I am inquiring from Father Wahl the list of the families who have
shown interest in sponsoring Vietnamese families in South Carolina.
I see that your preference is for a place in the City of Charleston.
I will do all I possibly can to explore such an opening and promptly
I will be in touch with you about the matter.

I am impressed with your description of your family and also of
your career. I was most attracted to the pictures of your family.
Your family would be a great asset to the Catholic community here
in Charleston.

When our Chairman, Father Wahl, communicates with me, I will
attempt to do all I can to make it possible for you to come to
Charleston; however, as you know, before I can do that, I must
have firm commitments from persons who will carry through such
a responsibility.

With friendly wishes and a blessing for you and your wonderful
family, I remain

Sincerely yours in Christ,

+ (Most Rev.) Ernest L. Unterkoefler
Bishop of Diocese of Charleston

Mr. Le-Cong-Chinh
Section 1, Tent E 11
Eglin AFB, Florida 32542

Reply letter from Bishop Ernest

CHAPTER SIX

Charleston, SC.

My Dad said, "Charleston is cold and we would need to dress appropriately." So, as we left the nearly 100 degree August weather of Florida, we put on sweaters and jackets.

Huy Hoàng and Hà were sweating under their sweaters and the overcoats that my Mom made them put on for the short two-hour flight to Charleston. My Mom and Dad too were sweating and kept wiping the sweat off their foreheads, but they could not wipe off the huge smiles that were on their faces.

We landed at Charleston Regional Airport around noon. There were no protesters this time; instead, Father Charles Rowland, the Chancellor of the Charleston Diocese, photographers and a dozen parishioners were there to welcome us.

My Dad shook hands with Father Rowland and the folks, and we queued up behind him, not knowing what to say or how to say it. The cameras kept flashing, so we smiled politely and nodded our heads saying *Thank-you*, while taking off our sweaters and jackets. It was very hot there too!

Father Rowland loaded us into a van and drove us to our new home, approximately fifteen minutes from the airport. During the drive, Father Rowland tried to make small talk with my Dad, but all my Dad could say was *Thank-you*. Charleston, South Carolina, was a small town near the Atlantic Ocean. Our new home was outside of town in a section called Charleston Heights. When we arrived, it was hot and humid, but the leaves on the trees had started to turn yellow, causing a rainbow of colors along the roads.

S. Vietnamese Family Overwhelmed By Hospitality

Father Rowland Greets Vietnamese Family At Airport

The arrival of our family in Charleston, South Carolina

My Mom cried as we shuffled into the simple house on a quiet street next door to St. John's School and St. John's Catholic Church, just outside of the Charleston Naval Base. The charming old house on cinder blocks with huge oak trees all around sat well back from the street. It was newly renovated, and the smell of paint still lingered in the air. There was food in the pantry and refrigerator, and clothes hanging in the closets. The house was fully furnished, and best of all, there was a window air conditioning unit and hot water that came out of the faucet. The simple house was certainly not the palatial high rise with chandeliers and fine furniture that my Mom used to have in Vietnam, but it was many times better than a tent in the refugee camps.

My Dad shook Father Rowland's hand repeatedly and kept saying Thank-you, as we sat down on the sofa and took off more and more layers of jackets and sweaters. The nuns of St. John's School, Sister Carol and Sister Sharon, were also there to welcome us and showed us how to use the appliances. They spoke slowly to my Mom and Lêvi, but I do not think they were listening or if they were, they didn't understand.

The house belonged to the people of St. John's Parish and was previously used as a temporary library for St. John's parochial school next door. It had three small bedrooms, one bathroom, a small kitchen with a backdoor, a modest dining room and living room. Mom and Dad took one of the smaller bedrooms, my three sisters shared the larger bedroom, and Huy Hoàng and Hà shared the smallest one in the middle. Since the house was quite small for all of us, the Parish also gave us a small adjacent space that was used for meetings. The boys used that space as our common bedroom.

St. John's School was a private Catholic school that housed less than 200 students. Sister Carol and five other nuns ran the school, and unlike the nuns in Vietnam, Sister Carol and her nuns wore normal everyday clothes. Their hair was short and they wore a small cross; otherwise, no one could tell they were nuns. They were much nicer than their Vietnamese counterparts..

The Pastor of St. John's Catholic Church, Father Joseph Tabone, came by to greet us. Father Tabone was a small man with a European accent. He smoked a pipe and always seemed to smile. My Dad told him that Hưng and I had attended seminaries in Vietnam, so he enlisted us to be altar boys for the church. St. John's church was a small church that could seat no more than 120 parishioners, but it was quite solemn and graceful. The church connected to the rectory, where Father Tabone resided, and it had a community hall on the other side for meetings. In front of the church, there was a small dirt parking lot.

When our guests and benefactors left, my Mom and Dad were exhausted. Here we were: No money, no jobs, no language skills. And now we owed a big debt to the people of St. John's Parish. My Mom cried. I could not tell if they were tears of self-pity or of happiness that we had made it out of Vietnam alive and survived the refugee camps. But I knew that my parents must be thinking about how to make a living and raise all of us kids in the new land called America.

On Sunday, Father Tabone introduced us to the people of the parish during the mass. We stood up from the front pews, turned around facing the congregation and bowed our heads to them. The parishioners clapped their hands in welcome. Later on after mass, they came to say hello to us, as we smiled and politely nodded our heads, not sure of what they had said.

Over the next several days, the people of the parish stopped by the house and dropped off donations of money, food, clothes, toys, bicycles, used furniture, and someone even gave me a BB gun. An owner of a nearby furniture store, at the urging of Father Tabone, offered my Dad a job, which my Dad gladly accepted. The following day, my Dad stood by the curb in front of our house at seven in the morning and a white Chevy pickup truck stopped and picked him up right on time. My Dad jumped onto the bed of the truck, smiled and waved good-bye to us as we watched from inside the house. The job of hauling and delivering furniture was hard on my Dad, as he was lean and thin; but it paid $2.10 an hour. And we needed the money.

The following week, we had a big surprise. Bishop Ernest had granted my Dad's request and sponsored my oldest brother Hùng out of the Fort Chaffee Refugee Camp, and now he was finally coming home to be with us in our new house in Charleston. As Father Rowland walked in the house with Hùng following closely behind him, my Mom rushed to embrace him. She held him for a long time and kept saying that she was sorry for making him stay behind on that fateful day in late April. She was crying tears of happiness. My Dad patted him on the back and we all surrounded him shouting out questions about how he had escaped Saigon.

He told us stories of how he fled Vietnam, made his way to Wake Island, then to the camp at Arkansas, where he found my Dad's messages. My Mom and Dad were very thankful to the Bishop for having brought Hùng home.

One of the parishioners who was familiar with US social services helped us fill out paperwork for food stamps. The food stamps were a great help to us. One day, we went to the nearby Winn-Dixie to buy some groceries. And since we did not have much money, we usually bought whatever was cheapest. I walked by an aisle and saw some pre-cooked canned meat, beef and chicken. On each can, it said "For the real meat lovers." We thought that sounded pretty good and loaded up our basket and brought them home.

My poor Mom did her best to prepare the food, but it did not taste right, and we could not believe Americans would eat something like this.

Later on, when one of the parishioners came over to see how we were doing, she looked at the cans that we bought and asked where our dog was? We did not have one, we told her, and she just broke down laughing so hard. It turned out that those canned meats were made by Alpo for dogs. We laughed with her too but did not really find it all that amusing. After that day, the nuns took time to give us English lessons.

Meanwhile, we went to work and school. The people of the parish heard about Hùng, and someone gave him a job at a grocery store called Red and White, where he stocked shelves and earned $1.80 an hour. My brother was a hard worker. Everyday, he rode his bicycle across two major highways and a bridge to go to work, rain or shine. Then at night, he went to a nearby technical college.

My older sister Lêvi, who was formerly an excellent student at the University of Saigon studying pre-med, found work as a live-in nanny for a wealthy young couple in downtown Charleston. These kind people encouraged my sister to continue her education and she enrolled at the College of Charleston in pre-med studies. She came home every other weekend.

My brother Hưng went to Bishop England High School near downtown Charleston, a private Catholic school full of rich kids, but Bishop Ernest got him in for free. In the morning, Hưng waited by the curb, and some parish kids would give him a ride to school. After school, he took the bus to work at a Piggly-Wiggly near downtown. And then after the store closed he took the bus home to Charleston Heights late at night. My brother Hưng spoke English well and was a hard worker; he worked seven days a week, and in a very short time, he was promoted to cashier. During that time, he stayed in touch with his Vietnamese girlfriend who had relocated from the refugee camp to Pensacola, Florida.

Although I had completed eighth grade at An-Phong, my parents asked me to retake eighth grade at St. John's school to learn English. Later I found out the true reason for my retaking eighth grade was so that my Mom and Dad would not burden the Bishop with the expensive tuition for my brother and me to attend Bishop England High School. So I was enrolled in eighth grade, my sister Huyền was in seventh, and my other sister Huyên (Tí) was in fifth at St. John's. The parish provided us free schooling, and after school each day, Huyền and I performed janitorial work. The nuns were pleased with our work and gave my parents $200 a month.

We worked hard and pooled our money to help my parents. My Mom still cried all the time, as she could not deal with cooking and taking care of eight kids. Back in Vietnam, she had servants to help with cooking, babysitting and general housework; so feeding us daily was a major effort for her. We did not have a car then, so occasionally one of the nuns took my parents to the grocery store to buy food and household supplies. Other times, we lined up and walked single file to the nearest Winn-Dixie about three miles away to buy food.

One day during our first winter in the US, our little house could not keep us warm. Hà was about one, and she came down with a severe fever. My Mom put vapor rub medicine *(dầu cù là)* on her, and gave her aspirin, but they didn't help. Hà's fever kept getting worse and the whole family was very concerned. My Dad and I went to the Eckerd Drug store next to the old Winn-Dixie late at night when the store was about to close. Dad struggled hard to tell the clerk what he needed, but the lack of vocabulary was so overwhelming that the clerk became frustrated and treated us like troublemakers he would just as soon be rid of.

My Dad, now forty-five-years old, a former commander of thousands of men, was on the verge of tears trying to communicate to save his daughter, while I could only stand there helplessly. All he wanted was to purchase a drug for Hà's fever. An old lady walked by and stopped to listen in on the conversation. Somehow she understood, and she told the clerk to give us what we were looking for. My Dad bought the medicine and we walked home in silence. I knew he was thanking God for sending him an angel.

Shortly thereafter, my Dad bought our first car. It was a very used white Plymouth Alliance for $200 cash. The old beat-up car had rusted through all around the outside and inside there was only the driver's seat. The trunk opened right into the inside of the car, so we put plywood on the passenger side and backseat floor areas. On top of the plywood, we laid blankets so the dust would not stream into the car when travelling on a dirt road. Gasoline was only 29 cents a gallon at the time and the old car was a true blessing for our family. We no longer had to walk to the grocery stores in the cold weather anymore, and my Dad did not have to wait in the cold everyday for the white truck. He now could drive to work.

With my Dad making $2.10 an hour, our family of ten was truly struggling. We worked and saved every penny. On the weekends, some parish folks would pick me up to do yard work. After I had cut the grass, trimmed the edges and weeded the flower beds, they would give me five dollars and perhaps a can of Coke. I would gulp down the soft drink and when I got home I gave my Mom the five bucks that I had earned. My brothers and sisters did the same thing. We gave her everything, even the tips in coins.

We were poor, but my Mom made sure we had enough to eat. Not fancy and expensive food, but we ate lots of fish and chicken. One time Sister Carol took my Mom to the supermarket and my Mom picked up a package of steaks to see how much they were, and then she lightly put it back down. Sister Carol saw that and insisted that she buy it for us. That act of kindness and so many other good deeds on our behalf are forever etched in our minds, and we owe much to the Bishop of Charleston, the Most–Reverend Ernest Unterkoefler and the good people of Charleston.

Bishop Ernest, as we called this gentle giant of a man, had mobilized his people, sponsored us and opened up his heart. He and his diocese paid our electric, gas, water, telephone and educational bills. They helped us completely and unconditionally. Their love and kindness taught us volumes about American generosity.

One day, while visiting our modest home, Bishop Ernest noticed that our air conditioning and heater were not working properly. The next day, he had the unit replaced with a brand new one. Throughout our stay in Charleston, it was the grace of God acting through the hearts of the good people of the parishes that had given us faith in the American People.

Another blessing for us was that we lived next door to St. John's church. The presence of God was a constant in our lives from Vietnam to America. We went to church as often as we could, and I made a point to go everyday at seven o'clock in the evening. It reminded me of my previous life at the seminary and it gave me peace. I served as altar boy and on Saturdays, I mowed and edged the lawn to make it look good for weekend services. The Catholic Youth Organization (CYO) invited me to join them, but my English was still too poor to participate.

Three times a week, my sisters and I took the bus to Charleston Community College to learn English as a second language (ESL) with a class of foreigners. English was a difficult language to master, but we were determined to learn it in order to keep up with our classmates in school. My sisters picked up the language much more easily and quickly than I did. One day, my Mom bought a 13-inch black and white RCA TV from the nearby K-Mart for us, and that greatly sped up our learning of the language. For us kids, our favorite shows were *Donny and Marie, Happy Days* and *Wild Wild West*. I particularly liked *Star Trek*, while my Mom loved wrestling. My older brothers were too busy to watch TV, so they listened to the Eagles and the Rolling Stones.

During the first winter, my Dad got a better paying job. The Public Works Department Solid Waste Plant outside of town needed a trash sorter, and they paid $2.44 an hour. Language skills were not needed, so my Dad signed up and got the job. His job was to sort out the garbage that the big trash trucks collected from people's houses. His workplace was stinky, and his station at the feeding end of the conveyor belt was disgusting. Everyday after work, he went directly to the shower upon getting home to wash up before dinner; otherwise no one could eat because the stench lingering on his clothes was so bad. But that was my Dad. He sacrificed so all of us could get ahead.

One morning, Dan Rather, the CBS-Television national news anchorman, showed up at our house with his entourage of cameramen to do a report on my Dad. He called it: *"Former Lieutenant Colonel of South Vietnam became a trash pickup man in the US."*

From Commander to Trash-Sorter

They filmed us in the little house as we were eating a breakfast of bran cereal before school, then they followed my Dad's beat-up car to work. They taped him sorting putrid trash and it was such an ordeal that several times during the shoot the crew ran outside to vomit. On the 5 o'clock news on TV the next day, I saw a determined and proud man, my Dad, doing his work without shame to feed our family. I also saw Dan Rather's moist eyes reporting our struggle, and I wondered if he was touched by what we were going through. Did the stink of my Dad's workplace, where he went day after day without complaint, get to the great newsman?

After the report was aired, my Dad was promoted to a better position at the Solid Waste Department and he was allowed to drive the big bulldozer at a landfill. While the smell from the landfill was no less offensive than that of his previous job, the open air made it somewhat more bearable.

Our first Christmas in the US was humble. Instead of a lighted Christmas tree with presents underneath as we always had back in Vietnam, we ate fried chicken and watched wrestling on a small black and white TV after church. My Mom and Dad promised us better days ahead and we believed them.

By the Vietnamese New Year Tết in February of 1976, my Mom bought us another car, a Dodge Polara for $500. It was a large car complete with front and back seats, a radio and air conditioning. My brother Hùng no longer had to ride his bike in the cold anymore to go to work and school. He could also take us to the market without waiting for my Dad to get home. We were still poor, but we no longer needed food stamps.

In May, for my graduation from St. John's school, my Mom took me to K-Mart and bought me my first suit: a polyester baby blue three piece suit on sale for $20. I wore it to the graduation ceremony in St. John's church, and was surprised to have won the American Legion Award for outstanding student that school year. Everyone in church gave me a standing ovation, which made my parents so proud and touched me deeply. While I was on Dượng Hưng's ship, I had silently prayed to make my friends and teachers at An-Phong Seminary proud of me and hoped that at this moment I had fulfilled my promise.

That summer, my brother Hưng got me a job at Piggly-Wiggly bagging groceries. My Mom bought Hưng a small Ford Capri so he could drive us both to work everyday. The customers loved Hưng and the grocery store owner gave him raises and complimented his work all the time. Meanwhile, my sister Lêvi continued babysitting and going to college and then started to work at a Chinese restaurant on the edge of town to further help the family.

My Mom and Dad kept in touch with the families of Cậu Năm and

Dượng Bảy, and let us know that they too were doing well and our cousins were growing strong and becoming good students. My Mom and Dad also found more relatives and friends throughout the country, and they communicated by mail and short phone calls. To keep informed of what was going on within the Vietnamese communities throughout the US, my parents subscribed to Vietnamese news magazines.

One year after Vietnamese refugees first arrived in America, and despite the efforts of the American refugee agencies to scatter the refugees all over the country, large Vietnamese communities sprung up in major cities in California, Texas, Virginia, Washington, Florida and New York. Louisiana became the main hub of commerce for expatriated Vietnamese. An American study found that more than 250,000 Vietnamese had made it to the US; the majority were trained in the medical professions or in technical or managerial occupations, and 70 percent of Vietnamese refugees came from urban areas of Vietnam. The study revealed that Vietnamese grocery stores, shops, doctors' offices, restaurants and law offices were providing services in their native language for refugees.

Being a true entrepreneur, my Mom dreamed of moving us to a larger town where she could get involved with the Vietnamese community and perhaps even do some commerce. She talked to Dì Bảy and Cậu Năm about moving together, but they quickly talked her out of it. Cậu Năm felt obligated to his sponsor and the Christian Brothers, and didn't want to move again. Dượng Bảy had a good job, and with young children, he preferred to stay in cold Cincinnati than move anywhere else. My Mom reluctantly put her ideas about moving on hold.

During our second year in the US, our family continued to work hard and study hard as before. My brother Hùng, while attending technical college, found a job as a mechanic's assistant and saved his money. Lêvi was doing really well in pre-med school and continued to work at the Chinese restaurant. Hưng and I attended Bishop England and worked at Piggly-Wiggly. Huyền was still at St. John's school and now she had help from my Mom who continued doing janitorial work after school. Tí babysat the two little ones and helped out as much as she could. Huy Hoàng and Hà were growing strong, healthy and happy.

In May of 1977, Huyền graduated from St. John's school and won more academic awards than the rest of her classmates combined. She was the star of the evening, as her classmates and their parents surrounded and congratulated her. Our family was so proud of her, and my Mom cooked a special meal to celebrate.

We all did well that year. My Mom bought Hùng a new Oldsmobile Cutlass Supreme and paid for it in cash. It was an awesome car, fully loaded with power steering, air conditioning, AM/FM/Cassette stereo, automatic windows, and the works. He thoroughly deserved it. My Dad retired the old Plymouth and took the Dodge to work. We also started to know the town and the surrounding areas better, so we went to the beach on weekends. Other times, we went out to catch crabs and clams. We even took Huy Hoàng and Hà to the drive-in movies, where they had a blast eating popcorn and watching movies while sitting on the hood of the Dodge Polara. Things were getting better and it was much more fun now that we understood more of the English language.

One night during our third year in Charleston, while we were all sleeping with the windows opened for fresh air, someone reached in and grabbed our small black and white TV sitting near the window in the living room. My Dad woke up because of the noise and chased the guy down the street. I heard the commotion, grabbed my BB gun and ran after my Dad and the thief. Soon my Dad and I found ourselves about a mile down the road from our house in the center of a bad neighborhood. Scary looking people came out of their houses and stared at us, so we retreated back to our house. This incident encouraged us to start looking elsewhere to live.

County of Charleston

Charleston, South Carolina
August 6, 1976

SOLID WASTE DISPOSAL PLANT
13 ROMNEY STREET
CHARLESTON, S. C. 29403

TO WHOM IT MAY CONCERN:

Mr. Chinh C. Le has been associated with Charleston County as an employee of the Solid Waste Reduction Center since November 3, 1975. As an employee of the Solid Waste Reduction Center, he has shown great ability to perform any duty assigned to him.

It is with much regret that I accept his resignation and I am sure that our loss will be someone else's gain.

I wish Mr. Le much success in his future employment and should he ever seek employment with Charleston County again he would be accepted without hesitation provided there is an opening.

Sincerely,

Lenard Singletary

Lenard Singletary, Manager
Solid Waste Reduction Center

LS/km

Recommendation letter for my Dad from Lenard Singletary of the Solid Waste Department

CHAPTER SEVEN

Houston, Texas

Shortly after the New Year of 1978, Dad's relative, Anh Trưởng, convinced him that Houston was the up and coming place to be.

Anh Trưởng was a young man of many talents, one of which was his uncanny ability to sell. He and his young wife lived in Pasadena, Texas, with seven very young children. He worked for one of the chemical plants but socialized with many Vietnamese people in Houston. When he found out that our family was living in Charleston, he called and promised to find a job for my Dad in Houston. Initially, my Dad hesitated. He felt obligated to the fine people of St. John's Parish, to Father Tabone, Sister Carol and other Sisters, Bishop Ernest and many other kind folks that had helped our family upon our arrival in the US. My Dad was concerned about uprooting us again after only a few years of settlement, and he also worried about the costs of living in a large town like Houston.

My Mom pointed out that we did not own the house we were living in so we were not tied down with a mortgage, and that our future might be better in a big town with better schools and more opportunities. Mom and Anh Trưởng did not have to persuade my Dad too much about Houston.

Houston was the fourth largest city in the US, and the weather for most of the year was hot and humid, just like that of Saigon. Vietnamese immigrants loved it there. To many of us, Houston was our second migration since coming to the US. Besides the warm weather, the multicultural aspects of this town enabled the Vietnamese to fit in instantly. Basic necessities, such as food, housing and gas, were inexpensive compared to the rest of the nation. Schools were relatively good for a major US city, and employment was reasonably attractive.

In 1978, there were at least 50,000 Vietnamese in Houston, most of us involved with the petroleum industry on the east side of town. The oil and gas refineries hired many Vietnamese, and the rest were scattered throughout town doing retail and clerical work. The Vietnamese opened up shops, such as restaurants, tailoring outlets, beauty salons, music media stores, doctors' and dentists' offices, lawyers' offices and other retail stores near downtown Houston and Houstonians called the area "Little Saigon."

Anh Trưởng told my Dad to drive down to Houston where he introduced him to Ali, the District Manager of Southland Corporation, who needed people to run 7-Eleven convenience stores. He hired Dad on the spot to run the cash register at one of his stores while Dad temporarily lived at Anh Trưởng's apartment in Pasadena, Texas. Ali later found out that my Dad was an Army officer who could manage much larger operations and signed him up for management training. And my Dad loved it.

Upon completing the course, Ali gave my Dad one of his 7-Eleven stores to manage. It was customary to give new managers the toughest stores to test their managerial ability, so Ali gave my Dad a small store located in a terrible neighborhood. My Dad did well, but he had to work many long hours to keep the store from being robbed, and merchandise and cash from being stolen by customers and employees.

My Dad called my brother Hùng to come down to help, and Hùng packed up his stuff and drove down in his Oldsmobile. Then my Dad rented a small one bedroom apartment next to the store, and together my Dad and Hùng took turns working 24-hours a day, seven days a week for several months straight. The hours were long, but the money was good. And besides, my Dad no longer had to work outside at the smelly solid waste landfill.

My brother Hưng was a freshman at the College of Charleston and was still working at Piggly-Wiggly to pay for his college education. Since it was summer vacation, my Mom urged him to go down to Houston and help out, so he left his job, said good-bye to his college friends, packed up his belongings, and drove his Ford Capri down to Houston and worked with my Dad and Hùng for several months at the 7-Eleven store.

Like other convenience stores, 7-Eleven served the local community by offering items such as coffee, beer, soft drinks, cigarettes, candies, small household items, and some stores sold gasoline. The stores were located throughout town, some in better neighborhoods than others; but most were managed by people with poor education, foreigners with limited language skills, or families of lesser means. The jobs were not difficult and involved handling the cash register, stocking merchandise, filling the coolers, and keeping the store clean.

There were usually three shifts: the early shift was from 7 (thus the first part of the name) to 3 o'clock; the second shift started at 3 and went to 11 (the second part of the name); and the night shift began at 11 and ended at 7 in the morning of the following day. It's not surprising that 7-Eleven stores in bad neighborhoods got robbed more regularly than those in better neighborhoods, but they all got robbed at one time or another. And the stores in poor neighborhoods had merchandise shoplifted more than those in richer areas. Generally, convenience stores were perfect for hard working Vietnamese families like ours with limited English skills who did not mind the long hours.

My Dad and older brothers lived in the one bedroom apartment next door and worked long days and nights at the store. My Dad worked the early shift, and after Hưng came to work, Dad did the paperwork, restocked the coolers, and helped Hưng keep watch on the store. He then went home to rest, and Hùng would come in and the two brothers worked until dark before Hưng went home to wake

Dad up to go to work. Everyday, the cycle repeated, so that at any given time, there were two people working in the store.

One day, when Hưng had already gone home for the night, and Dad hadn't arrived yet, a guy walked in the store and demanded that Hùng sell him beer after hours. My brother refused and the man yelled racial slurs and trashed the store. When Hùng insisted that he leave, he stormed out cursing.

Shortly, he returned, marched up to my brother, pointed a gun at his face and demanded beer and the money from the cash register. Hùng calmly put the money in a bag and gave it to the robber. He grabbed the bag and couple of six-packs, and then ran out of the store. Hùng called the police and reported the incident. When my Dad saw flashing lights from police cars in front of the store, he feared that something had happened to Hùng. From that day on, my Dad kept a handgun at the store and was never late again. He never told my Mom about the incident.

As the store my Dad managed became more profitable, Ali gave him a raise and promoted him to a larger store in a better neighborhood. This new store had heavier traffic, and all three of them had to work much harder. So my Dad called for reinforcements.

Lêvi was attending summer school in North Charleston and working at the Chinese restaurant at the edge of town in the evening. My Mom had just bought her a brand new Toyota Corolla for $2,000 cash, since Hưng had already taken his Ford Capri to Houston. Meanwhile I was working full-time at Piggly-Wiggly and doing yard work for St. John's church on weekends. My Mom had already told us about her plan to move to Houston, so we were already starting to pack our belongings and preparing our younger siblings for the move.

We were excited about the prospect of living in Houston, but we were also scared of this new unknown. I talked to Father Tabone and the new pastor of St. John's church, Father Leigh Lehocky, about our pending departure and they were sad to see us leave, but believed that Mom and Dad were doing the right thing for us. Sister Carol and Sister Sharon of St. John's School were also sad to see us go, and they sympathized with our wish to better ourselves and satisfy our longing to be with a larger Vietnamese community. Lêvi and I left Charleston early on a foggy Sunday morning, as my Mom, Huyền and the rest of the kids stood on the front porch of the old house waving good-bye.

Lêvi and I talked about many things during our 24-hour trip to Houston. In many ways, she and I were so much alike. We were both fiercely independent and strong minded, even when we were little kids in Vietnam. She was the oldest girl in the family, and while my Mom was too busy growing her business, Lêvi had to attend to herself and her younger siblings. Over time, she became street smart and wiser than her years.

One day back in the old country, Lêvi wrote my Mom a letter expressing how she felt suffocated by my Mom's overwhelming control of her life and yet lacking of support. She was eighteen-years-old then and had already started college. In the letter, she described my Mom as more repressive than the Việt Cộng. And she asked Mom to be gentler and loving like her sister Dì Bảy.

Well, while it might be acceptable in American culture to be so forthright, open and sincere about such matters, in our Vietnamese society, this bold and progressive action was greatly discouraged and was considered intolerable. My Mom was extremely upset with Lêvi and their relationship was never the same afterward. While my sister had not regretted writing such a letter, she was much more sympathetic to my Mom now after the refugee ordeal that we had gone through. Seeing my Mom going from riches to rags overnight made Lêvi more compassionate and appreciative of life in a Vietnamese family.

Lêvi told me how badly she felt for my Mom. My Mom, once an articulate, vibrant and successful entrepreneur in Vietnam, was now reduced to a helpless lady with no language skills, a misfit having a hard time adapting to the new culture. She remembered how powerful my Mom used to be when influential men and women of our old country solicited her help supporting their causes with her money and influence. Lêvi told me about how my Mom was able to make real estate deals all over the country and of her goals for amassing more wealth to pass down to us. My Mom always had big dreams for each one of us kids.

As a typical Vietnamese mother, my Mom wanted to have at least one doctor and one priest in the family, and was hoping that Lêvi would become a doctor and that Hưng or I would become a priest. She wished that all of us would be able to finish college and do well in life. She wanted lots and lots of grandchildren, and my Mom worked hard to realize her dreams while in Vietnam.

Coming to America changed everything for her. She was no longer the powerful lady that she once was. There were no maids, no elegant residences, no fancy cars and no circle of high society friends anymore. In fact, besides the families of Cậu Năm and Dượng Bảy, she had few Vietnamese friends in the small town of Charleston. She found the English language difficult to learn. While the written words were not that complicated, the pronunciation sometimes did not make sense to her. Besides, the Americans talked too quickly, as they always seemed to be rushed for time. So she infrequently left home or only went out with my Dad and us kids.

My Mom also was having a hard time adapting to the food here. All her life, rice and noodles were the basics for meals, but in Charleston, the rice that was sold at Winn-Dixie and Piggly-Wiggly was different and expensive. And while there was plenty of pasta noodles, there was no Vietnamese noodles to be found anywhere in Charleston.

Everyday back home, she had one of her maids go to Chợ Nancy (Nancy's open market) nearby and buy fresh meats, seafood and vegetables and prepare the meals for us. There was little need for massive refrigerators and pantries. But in Charleston, the nearest super market was three miles away, and everything was either in cans, plastic packages or Styrofoam trays. While it was convenient, nothing was fresh. Moreover, Americans used salt and pepper with everything, while the Vietnamese ate all things with an assortment of sauces. My Mom was at a loss for how to make regular meals using ingredients from the supermarkets. Lêvi and I prayed that over time our Mom would forget about her past glory and feel better about living in the US.

Then we talked about our own ambitions. Lêvi always wanted to be a dentist and have her own dental clinic. She felt that if she kept trying and studying hard, she would eventually become one and she would be able to make decent money to help our family. I asked her if that was what she really wanted or was it my Mom's wish that she was fulfilling. She said it was both. She then smiled softly as if trying to convince herself that she actually believed her own statement. Deep down inside, I knew my sister could do whatever she put her mind to. I just hoped that our financial situation would not hold her back.

Lêvi asked me about my aspirations, and I told her I wanted to be an architect. I wanted to design and build houses and buildings. I told her that I was fascinated by how quickly and efficiently Americans build houses, and even roads and bridges. Years and years of war had destroyed our old country. The infrastructure, if any, was badly designed and poorly maintained. Roads were full of potholes due to bombs and mines, and then worsened by monsoon rains, and bridges were unsafe for trucks and pedestrians.

The roads were in such poor shape that the transporting of materials to build houses and buildings could not be done with ease and efficiency. And I wanted somehow to help in the efforts to rebuild Vietnam. So I thought it was best for me to be an architect. Lêvi laughed and patted me on the head. She thought it was noble for a high school sophomore to have such dreams. I was just happy to share my thoughts with my sister, as we were driving down the interstate toward Houston.

Neither of us had left the State of South Carolina before, and we were intrigued by the sheer size of America. From Charleston, South Carolina, it took us more than three hours to get to Georgia's state line. It was early summer and the weather was getting warmer. The trees along the side of the road were green and the state of Georgia had rolling hills and huge oak trees everywhere. We drove through the charming City of Savannah with its plantations and enormous oak trees, and stopped at a little convenience store to get gas and some drinks.

The drive from Savannah to Jacksonville, Florida, was uneventful, but Jacksonville was the largest town that we had ever seen. We got there right before the evening rush hour, and the congestion had started. Highway 95 took us straight into downtown Jacksonville, and we were in awe of what we saw. The small two-lane Highway 95 from the outskirts of town opened up to six or seven lanes, with multi-level overpasses filled up with cars and trucks. The skyscrapers in the downtown area were colossal and we both gawked at the skyline, and as we got closer, we saw that an enormous river ran through the town. On the river banks, there were large transport ships docking and workers were busy loading and unloading cargo using huge cranes. The industrial complex was much larger than the one we saw in the Philippines, and we were both amazed by the modern facility. Farther down the river, barges and tugboats moved peacefully through the clear blue water. The scenery reminded us of the final days on the Saigon River, except this time we were safe in a peaceful country.

Interstate Highway 10 met up with IH-95 near downtown, and we took I-10 west. I told Lêvi that one day, I would come back and visit this beautiful town. The small Toyota Corolla was doing well on the road. It was just a barebones basic stick shift car, but it was the first car that I helped my Mom buy.

One day my Mom saw an ad on TV, and the announcer said that for $2,000, we could own a brand new Toyota Corolla. The next day, I went with her to the bank and watched her withdraw $2,000 in cash and put the money in a paper bag. Then we went directly to the car dealer. Since my Mom did not speak English, she told me to tell the salesman that she wanted to buy the $2,000 car that she had seen on TV. The old car salesman said that there was no such car, but my Mom insisted that she saw it on television so it had to be true.

She persisted and he finally showed us a no-frills basic Corolla, and my Mom said that was it. She wanted to buy that one. Taxes, title and licenses added up to about $2,200. My Mom only had $2,000 and she insisted that the man on TV said for $2,000 we could own a brand new Corolla. So I played interpreter and mediator for another hour before the old salesman broke down and yielded to my Mom's demand.

To the dismay of the sales manager, my Mom took $2,000 in cash out of the paper bag and proceeded to count the bills, one by one, in front of the man. They rushed us to the back office, counted the money and gave my Mom the keys to her brand new Toyota Corolla. My Mom smiled triumphantly as we drove off the lot with the car she wanted. When we got home, she gave the keys to Lêvi and told her the car was hers. From that day on, Lêvi did not have to take the bus to school and to work anymore.

I told Lêvi about how Mom bought the car and we both had a good laugh. To this day, I still have not figured out if my Mom had intentionally played *me-no-English* and used me as a buffer, or if she truly did not know any better.

The car had an AM-FM radio, but we kept it off, because the radio signals kept fading in and out as we went down I-10. We pulled into a rest stop along the highway, and Lêvi let me take over and drive. I drove into the night as Lêvi fell asleep on the passenger side. It was peaceful driving at night. Except for the occasional 18-wheeler that whizzed by, the road was clear and silent. I-10 stretched out over the flat Florida landscape between Jacksonville and Tallahassee, so the drive was quite boring, but it gave me much time to think. I missed my friends in Vietnam and the hustle of Saigon. The roads back home were bad compared to those in the US, but they were full of life with people on their scooters honking their horns, swerving around potholes, and veering in and out of traffic. There were red lights at intersections, but no one ever paid attention to them. People yielded to people in organized chaos.

One day in Vietnam, my brother Hung and I were crossing the Street of Trần Hưng Đạo. The traffic was quite heavy, but we inched our way forward. As we got to the middle of the street, a three-wheeled Lambretta, a sort of very small bus that would pick up people for a small fare, swerved to avoid hitting us. A young man on a Honda scooter turned quickly to avoid hitting the Lambretta and instead he hit my brother squarely on his side. The force of the accident threw my brother into the air and he landed on top of me in the middle of the busy street. Hưng was badly bruised and had scratches up and down his arms. I was scared but all right.

The young man fell off his scooter and was very upset. He knew by the way we were dressed that we were two rich kids from a powerful family. He helped Hưng and me to the side of the street, and saw that Hưng was hurt and really mad. I pointed to our house and told the young man that we lived there, and that he should take Hưng home. The young man, probably no more than twenty, picked Hưng up and carried him to my house.

My Mom, Lêvi and the maids rushed down to tend to Hưng as the young man stood by with tears in his eyes. Even though the accident wasn't his fault, he was terrified of what might happen to him. My Mom inspected Hưng and found that he was black-and-blue, but otherwise uninjured except for a few minor abrasions. She then called the young man over and lectured him on how he must be careful on a busy street; then she let him go. No insurance, no police, and no hassle. For the next several days, the young man came back to our house everyday to check up on Hưng and even brought him candy.

Hưng was just fine and I knew the guy was more interested in checking out Lêvi than any of us. Too bad for him that Lêvi did not think he was her type. Those were the ways of my old country, how potholes, scooters, and crossing busy streets could lead to chance meetings. In contrast, the massive concrete highways of the new land seemed impersonal, cold and lonely. The *Eagles'* lyrics of the song named *Desperado* …

> " …And freedom, oh freedom, well, that's just some people talkin'; your prison is walking through this world all alone …"

… seemed so meaningful as we drove along through the empty night. I missed the clamor and bustle of a busy Saigon.

In the earlier hours of the following morning, we drove past the old Eglin Air Force Base. It seemed so long ago that we had stayed there, and I wondered how much things had changed at the Base. I was most certain that they had folded up the tents of the refugee camps, yet I felt disappointed that that chapter of history would not be memorialized by some statue or annual ceremony. I suppose it was one of the dark episodes of our lives that everybody wished to forget. Yet it was a critical part of my life and the lives of thousands of expatriate Vietnamese. It was our gateway to America.

The sun rose lazily behind us as we continued heading west toward Texas. After we stopped to get gas and a breakfast of Twinkies from a gas station outside of Mobile, Alabama, Lêvi took over the driving. I had a quick nap and woke up as we got to Baton Rouge, Louisiana. We stopped for lunch at a small restaurant and gave the Corolla a rest. The gumbo and French bread were so good in Louisiana and Lêvi and I were so hungry that we swallowed the whole meal in minutes. I made a mental note to come back to Louisiana as often as I could. After lunch, we felt refreshed and ready for the last leg of our trip. I took over the driving and Lêvi told me about how much she missed her friends in Vietnam.

Her best friend was a girl named Thanh. They had known each other since junior high school at Thánh Linh, and practically grew up together. We called her Thanh Đen (Dark Thanh), because her skin color had a darker tone. She came from a poor family where her father worked as a civilian for the South Vietnamese Government, and her mother worked off and on doing housework for wealthy families in Saigon. Thanh Đen had sad eyes but a cheerful smile—when she smiled. Lêvi and Thanh Đen came from opposite ends of Vietnamese society, but they were the best of friends. My sister was much brighter and often helped Thanh Đen with her homework; however, Thanh Đen was much more of a romantic and kept my sister educated on why boys did what they did. Together they had fun and loved each other dearly.

Thanh Đen often came over to our house and hung out with my sister. They went everywhere together on my sister's Honda scooter. After high school, my sister went directly to college to study pre-medicine. Thanh Đen was less fortunate; she did not do well on the baccalaureate tests, and did not get accepted into college. While my sister was attending college, Thanh Đen was unemployed and did odd jobs to get by.

They saw each other as often as they could. Before our departure from Saigon, my sister advised Thanh Đen to get her family prepared to leave the country, but her family did not or could not afford to go. On the day before our departure, Thanh Đen came by to say good-bye to my sister, and they cried and held onto each other.

Lêvi asked if Thanh Đen would like to go with us, but she declined. So they promised to keep in touch after things settled down. I remembered how hard my sister cried when Thanh Đen left the old house. Lêvi was sniffling now as she told me about her friend, and I sympathized with my dear sister. Like so many Vietnamese immigrants, I had lived through the same experience of leaving friends behind. The end of the war came so abruptly that good-byes were a seldom luxury for a lifetime of friendships. We drove in silence until we got to our new city of Houston.

My Dad was waiting for us at the corner of 45th and Calvacade, and we followed his Dodge Polara back to the apartment. My Dad seemed tired but he was happy to see we made it there safely. The following week, my Dad and two older brothers trained Lêvi and me on our new jobs. And during the week, my Dad rented a larger two bedroom apartment on 34th Street in preparation for moving the rest of our family to Houston. On Sunday, my Dad and Hưng drove the Polara back to Charleston.

On June 1st of 1978, our family moved into the new apartment in Houston, Texas. It was so nice to see our family reunited again, even though the apartment was too small for the ten of us. Actually, at the most only eight of us were home at any given time, since two would be working at the 7-Eleven on Calvacade. My Mom and Dad plus Huy Hoàng and Hà took one bedroom, the three girls took the other one, and my brothers and I took turns sleeping on the sofa or on the floor of the living room whenever we got off work.

It turned out that my parents loved Houston and the new friends that they made. On Sundays after church, they went out to see their friends and other distant relatives in town. At other times, they went to the Vietnamese supermarket on Milam Street near downtown Houston to buy ethnic Vietnamese food.

My Dad continued to do a good job managing 7-Eleven stores, and the four of us older kids worked hard so Dad would be assigned better stores to manage. My Dad's supervisor Ali was impressed by our family's work ethic and kept promoting my Dad every other quarter. My oldest brother Hùng enrolled in a technical school in pursuit of his mechanic's license. Lêvi and Hưng registered at the University of Houston. Lêvi was continuing her pre-med studies, and Hưng was in Business. Huyền and I signed up at Waltrip High School in Northwest Houston. My parents put Tí and Huy-Hoàng in a private Catholic grade school called Christ the King on North Main Street. And Hà stayed home with my Mom. We all worked hard and studied hard that first year in Houston. And 7-Eleven was good to my Dad and our family.

One night I was working the late shift with my Dad. He really liked assigning me to the late shift because he knew that I would load up the walk-in cooler so it would last for days. Then I would reorganize the stock to make it clear for access, empty the cartons and clean up the store. I usually dry-mopped the store first, then I would mop it with hot water twice, and then apply wax on the final pass. I had done something similar to this many times before when Huyền and I cleaned St. John's school. That night, as always, I did my cooler and floor duties, then I took a little break.

About 2:30 in the morning, a short guy with dark hair wearing a raincoat came into the store. He crossed to the cooler to get beer, but I had locked it at midnight. Frustrated, he went to the sandwich cooler near the cashier's aisle. I said hello and tried to make small talk, but he did not respond and was avoiding looking straight at me.

After several minutes, he left the store, looking annoyed. I thought it was unusual, but did not wake up my Dad who was sleeping on a cot in the storage room. The same man came back a half hour later. This time he walked straight up to me at the cash register and demanded money. He opened up the raincoat just enough to show me the dark barrel of a handgun he was holding.

The .45 caliber automatic was shaking in his hand. He was jumpy and scared, probably as much as I was. I told him to calm down and that I would reach for a paper bag to put the money in. He looked around, nodding his head, as I opened the cash register, took out the cash and stuffed it in the bag. He grabbed the bag quickly from my hand and rushed to the door.

He slammed hard into the left door, as we always locked the left door after midnight and kept the right door open. I looked at the tape measure along the side of the door; it said that he was 5'5." The guy seemed embarrassed, cracked a smile, opened the right door and disappeared into the night. I woke up my Dad and we called the police to file a report. Shortly after the incident, my Dad requested Ali to assign us to a new store at a better location.

In July of 1979, our family achieved the American Dream of owning our own home. My Mom bought us a house in Southwest Houston. The house was located in a middle class neighborhood, and it had four bedrooms, two baths, a kitchen, living room, dining room, family room and a detached two-car garage. It sat on a corner lot that came with a big backyard. We were elated to have a house that could accommodate all ten of us at the same time.

Meanwhile, my Dad was now so appreciated that he could select the 7-Eleven that he wanted to manage, so he chose a new store less than three miles from the house. Huyền and I transferred to Sharpstown Senior High School near our house. Tí, who had graduated with honors from Christ the King, was now going to another private Catholic school named St. Francis DeSale with Huy Hoàng and Hà.

On school days, Hùng, Hưng and Lêvi worked the first shift whenever their college class schedules allowed. After high school finished for the day, I handled the second shift, and my Dad worked the night shift. On the weekend, I worked one night shift and my brothers worked the other. The hours were long, but we were making money during a tough economic time in America.

Houston was good to us. The large population of Vietnamese immigrants meant a great selection of Vietnamese supermarkets, restaurants, shops, and service providers, and that translated into better Vietnamese foods, groceries, community services, churches and opportunities. It also meant more chances for young Vietnamese to meet and socialize. My sister Lêvi met and fell in love with a fellow Vietnamese student at U of H. His name was Sơn Nguyễn, and he came from a hardworking family living in a small town fifty miles southeast of Houston called Lake Jackson, also known as the home of Dow Chemical USA.

Sơn was the oldest son of a large family. His parents came to the US at about the same time that we had arrived. Their sponsor lived in Lake Jackson, so the family settled there as well. Like us, they were industrious and saved and pooled their money. They bought a Dennys' restaurant and converted it into the only Vietnamese-Chinese restaurant in town and did very well. Sơn majored in Chemical Engineering at the University of Houston, and that was where he met my sister Lêvi. The two of them made a good couple, and we all liked him.

My brother Hưng was also involved at U of H. He was good-looking, articulate and extremely sociable. He was an officer of the university's Vietnamese-American Student Organization, and the Vietnamese college girls were crazy about him. Hưng majored in Business Administration and wanted to run his own company one day.

My other brother Hùng completed his mechanic's certification in 1979 and was employed at a Toyota Dealership. He was a very good mechanic and loved what he was doing. Huyền and I attended Sharpstown High School and we were both at the top of our classes. After school, we worked at our Dad's 7-Eleven. There was no time for proms, dances or school related activities, but we were quite happy contributing to our family's growth and good fortune.

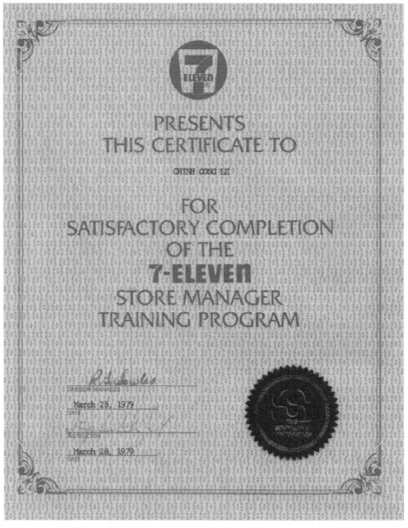

My Dad's 7-Eleven Store Manager Certificate

CHAPTER EIGHT

Five Years Later
1980

1980 was a tough year for the people of the United States. The Iran Hostage Crisis had consumed the hearts and minds of the Americans. President Jimmy Carter was failing to stop the rise of interest rates and home foreclosures as the economy worsened. There were long lines at gas stations even in Houston, and jobs were scarce, even for Vietnamese immigrants willing to do anything.

By the end of 1980, the number of Vietnamese in the US had reached more than 600,000. Then a second wave of Vietnamese migration began as the cruel regime of Communist Vietnam took its vengeance on the people of South Vietnam.

Major US cities with warmer climates attracted many Vietnamese, and as that population grew, it attracted many more. This time the Vietnamese population was no longer a drain on local resources, but brought life into many economically depressed areas.

In Houston, the slums at the southwest edge of downtown were revitalized with new Vietnamese shops and restaurants. At the same time, the Vietnamese took over the convenience store business with small family-operated stores: 7-Eleven, U-Totem, Stop-n-Go and others. With a stagnant economy and rising unemployment, many Houstonians started to resent our quiet growth. Their jealousy soon turned to admiration as their children were outscored in high schools and colleges by the children of Asian immigrants who could barely speak English when they arrived.

Far from the days of mass confusion at the end of the Vietnam War, when my Dad was tormented by his patriotic ideals and his sense of family obligation, he and my Mom were determined to take full advantage of the opportunities offered by the United States to raise their children to compete with the very best of Americans. He was now a man of peace, possessed by a sense of purpose, doing his best to help us build a better life for our family.

Since coming to America, he had worked hard. From sorting trash in the earlier days to managing a convenience store, he had tried to advance himself and elevate our family's standard of living. He had no time for distractions and had turned down many offers and pressures from other older Vietnamese to participate in local Vietnamese politics. Instead, he remained focused on running his store so his children could have time to study and do well in school.

Everyday, he went to the store and usually worked the nightshift so we wouldn't have to. If there was going to be a robbery, it would always happen at night and he wanted to protect us from danger. He had been robbed several times, but fortunately he had not been harmed. He dismissed the holdups as a deplorable but inevitable part of the job.

Except for the mandatory closing on Christmas Day, my Dad never took a day off. He worked every holiday including Tết and Thanksgiving, although we would take turns running the store so he could spend time at home enjoying the festivities. It saddened him greatly that, except for Christmas Day, for several years he was not able to join us at the dinner table.

He took great joy and pride in the fact that all of his children were doing well in school. He often said that wealth is intrinsic, if we have it *inside*, we are wealthy no matter what.

The one constant in his life and in ours was religion. My Dad went to church every Sunday and he made sure that we did, too. His other constant was my Mom. She was our family's master architect, the one who planned and built and cajoled us into reaching for a fulfilling and enriching future.

From the beginning of our lives here in the US, it was difficult for my Mom. For months, she cried and struggled while trying to adjust to the harsh life of being poor in a strange land. Once she accepted reality, her ambitious entrepreneurial spirit soared. In her mind, the land of opportunitiy was truly for us to profit, but this time instead of advancing her own enterprises, she was determined to build everything from scratch through the lives of her children. My Mom relentlessly pushed us to study harder, to work harder and to be our own persons. "We never had such chance in war torn Vietnam, and this is our chance now," she often said.

She had given up on her wish for Hưng and me to become priests and did not pressure us any more. Perhaps it was the American lack of respect for the holy profession compared to the high regard for priests in Vietnam. Nevertheless, she was proud of our modest achievements. She bragged to Cậu Năm, Dì Bảy and our relatives about each one of her children, yet she was careful not to do so in front of us. She wanted us to look ahead and try harder, and never look back and settle for what we had accomplished.

It comforted her to know that Cậu Năm's and Dì Bảy's families were doing exceptionally well, too. My Mom loved Houston, and since we moved into the new house, she was much happier. Houston offered her the luxury of Vietnamese foods and friends. It brought her closer to our customs and Vietnamese language. Every year, she prepared lavish feasts at Tết and gathered many friends and relatives to celebrate our tradition. She felt at ease and called Houston home.

My Mom was the glue that held us together. We worked and pooled our money, and my Mom was our treasurer. She paid all the bills and gave each of us what we needed. As a diehard entrepreneur, she urged Hưng to open his own business. She encouraged Lêvi and Huyền, while still in college, to dream about having their own clinics.

She was also a religious person. Just like in Vietnam, she went to church every Sunday, and then afterwards went to the supermarket to buy food and sundries. She made her routines as similar as she could to those she had known in Vietnam and we were glad she felt better about herself and her family.

The first five years in the US were tough on our family, but with our newfound American freedom and the prospects for riches, both inner and outer, our family adapted and grew. As my Dad used to say, "The foundation needs to be solid and strong, before we can build the house." Our family was building a new life in America on a solid foundation.

CHAPTER NINE

Cậu Năm

Friday, November 28, 2008

Cậu Năm was lying in bed. The house was dark and warm. Fever slowly cooked his frail body from inside. His sweat soaked the bed's wrinkled top sheet, and the cycles between his many chills and fevers worsened. The medicine he had taken an hour before played tricks on his mind and he wavered between dreams and reality.

As the only son in a large Vietnamese family, Cậu Năm was blessed and privileged. Ông Ngoại had loved him and spoiled him ever since he was little. His older sisters Dì Hai, Dì Ba and Dì Bốn adored him, and he ruled my Mom and Dì Bảy. Cậu Năm was a good-looking man, tall, with big brown eyes and a straight nose; he was well educated and very articulate. Just like Ông Ngoại, Cậu Năm was a strict disciplinarian and my almighty mother always behaved timidly around him.

Back in Vietnam, he was an administrator at the University of Nha Trang and a powerful man in the community. At a young age, he married Mợ Năm and had ten children, seven boys and three girls by the time he was forty. He was religious but strict with his kids. They loved him dearly but also feared his temper. When they fought among themselves or cursed out loud, they got a slap across the face.

Mợ Năm was a quiet and gentle lady. She was well educated and had taught high school in Nha Trang. Her kids adored her and were polite and proper. The boys were fun to be around and the girls were good-natured and shy.

Cậu Năm had worked for the Americans for several years and was fluent in English. His language skills had helped us considerably during our exodus from Vietnam and it enabled him to get a sponsor for his large family quite quickly, but his family life in the US was not going well.

The stress of raising a large family in the US had put a huge strain on him and his wife. He and his wife often fought, mostly about money and sometimes about raising the children. In the late '80s, Cậu Năm and Mợ Năm separated, and for a time, Cậu Năm moved to Houston and worked with my Dad at 7-Eleven. The two men became good friends and often went fishing together every other weekend.

Around 1990, Cậu Năm met an easygoing Vietnamese lady we called Cô Lisa, and he settled down with her in Houston. Being a devout Catholic, my Mom had an issue over his living arrangement, and after that Cậu Năm and my Mom rarely talked. However, they still loved each other, and Cậu Năm's situation did not stop my Dad from going fishing with him on weekends. My Mom often asked us to visit Cậu Năm and to be cordial, but for years Cậu Năm was a lonely man, as his ten children rarely visited him.

Whenever we saw Cậu Năm, he loved to talk about his

Cậu Năm in Galveston

fishing trips with my Dad and how he had persuaded my Mom to 'allow' Dad to go with him. He talked for hours about how he helped my Dad carry the coolers and fishing gear due to my Dad's poor health, about how he paid for gas because my Dad never had any money, and about how he always caught more fish than my Dad. Each time, Cậu Năm beamed with pride and confidence.

He was always so happy and boastful when talking about his children. He loved to be *"Ông Cố"* due to the ordination of Father Tân, his second son; he talked about his son-in-law Anh Danh and his oldest daughter Chị Dạ Thu with delight; and he bragged constantly about his youngest son Anh Quốc's education and free spirit. Depite his relentless enthusiasm, everyone loved Cậu Năm for his sharp mind and quick wit.

A slight stir threw Cậu Năm into a coughing fit. It shook his fragile body and contorted it into a ball of pain. He gasped for air as though he was about to drown. The fire in his lungs burned as each successive breath was harder to draw; his throat felt like sheets of sandpaper rubbing against each other. His eyes watered and his vision blurred. He felt nauseated and dizzy. He was about to black out, but the constant coughing kept him conscious. He coughed until there was no more air in his lungs to draw and he collapsed onto the soaked pillow.

In the living room, Anh Quốc paused in mid-sentence during our conversation, and we all listened tentatively.

"He'll be okay." Anh Quốc said quietly, lying with a heavy heart. "He is much better today. Yesterday the doctor took out more than a liter and a half of fluid from his lungs, and he can breathe better now."

My wife Dung and I looked at each other; we both knew what the buildup of fluid meant. Anh Quốc, who was a small man at five feet five and 115 pounds, suddenly looked much older from when we had seen him the week before. The ponytail was the same, but the polite smile seemed tired and worried.

About a week before, Cậu Năm's youngest son Anh Quốc came to visit. He was an accountant for a mid-size company in Missouri and was bored with his job. One day, he quit his job and became a driver for a trucking company. He wanted to be free and travel, he said; and he had been on the road for more than a year. On his most recent route through North Texas, he stopped in Houston to pay Cậu Năm a visit. Then someone stole his 18-wheeler with all his belongings inside, so he was stranded in Houston. Perhaps it was fate, but Anh Quốc decided to stay for a while to take care of his dad. His career had to wait and the lost truck was the least of his worries now.

He rushed to help Cô Lisa, who was struggling to help Cậu Năm sit up; but Cậu Năm insisted on getting out of bed. Anh Quốc carried Cậu Năm to the dining table. Cậu Năm seemed even more exhausted from the effort, but he was happy to see Dung and me there by his side. Cô Lisa brought him a small bowl of soup, and Anh Quốc made tea for him. A worn out Cậu Năm tried to make small talk while trying to catch his breath.

Cậu Năm recalled how funny it was when he first came down to Houston and visited us at our house. My youngest son Minh was only two, and he was hooked on his pacifiers. Although bright and alert, Minh did not want to talk. Instead he sucked his pacifier all day and only removed it to eat. Minh called his pacifier "wy," and he and his wy were inseparable.

Playfully, Cậu Năm would remove the wy from his mouth to force him to say something, but Minh would immediately pop another wy into his mouth. Then Cậu Năm yanked that one out, too, and then Minh shoved another one into his mouth. Cậu Năm and Minh would play this game several times until Minh ran out of pacifiers. Finally, Minh would give up and say something to please Cậu Năm and get all his pacifiers back. And then Minh would stuff his mouth with four or five of his wys, make faces at Cậu Năm and then run off. Cậu Năm smiled sadly and said how much he missed his children and grandchildren.

At seventy-five-years-old, Cậu Năm had ten children and twelve grandchildren. He loved them all but never had much time with them. The feud between him and Mợ Năm was long and often bitter.

Sometimes the situation became too much for him and he said and did hurtful things. He knew that he had caused great pain to his children who had grown up in an unhappy home.

In Vietnam, he and Mợ Năm worked hard but were able to adequately care for their ten children. He and Mợ Năm had their differences, but life was reasonably peaceful. His kids were young and the strict discipline he imposed was the norm for an autocratic Vietnamese family.

Life in the US was different and his harsh rules didn't work over here. As his children grew up more American than Vietnamese, the authoritarian ways of a Vietnamese father clashed with the American values of freedom and independence. His children came and went without asking permission and they said and did things without consulting him. He grew frustrated and unhappy over time and felt less important. Yet all through his frustration, he continued to love and pray for them.

My sister Tí came into the room, and Cậu Năm's eyes lit up. She had brought him communion practically everyday lately, and receiving communion was the highlight of Cậu Năm's day. The results from the medical labs had not yet come back, but he assumed there must be something seriously wrong because of the incessant coughing. For several months, the small nagging cough would not go away. And then, day after day, his appetite waned, and he lost a lot of weight.

His coughing had actually gotten worse and his lungs burned every time he coughed. On the last several Sundays, he could not gather enough strength even to go to church. Thank God for Ti'.

To see a man without fear come into peace with God was a humbling experience. I prayed that he would be well soon. Dung and I joined Tí, Cậu Năm, Anh Quốc and Cô Lisa at the table. Silently I asked God to have mercy on Cậu Năm; I prayed that God be gracious to His faithful and grant Cậu Năm peace; and to extend such peace to all of Cậu Năm's family. Then I asked God to give Anh Quốc and his siblings strength and courage in the days to come.

"Forgive us our trespasses, as we forgive those who trespass against us," I prayed. Tí gently gave Cậu Năm communion; such a simple and loving gesture brought tears to my eyes. I silently wished that I could have done the act of giving out Holy Communion, as my Dad had wished for me.

Cậu Năm was cheerful and talkative after receiving communion. His coughing seemed to subside somewhat; perhaps the small dinner gave him some comfort; perhaps it was the communion that eased his soul.

We sat in the living room and visited for a while. Cậu Năm seemed genuinely happy. Cô Lisa was cheerful too. She complained about how Cậu Năm would not eat and would not let her take care of him, but she was happy we were around to talk to the both of them. Anh Quốc sat quietly enjoying the conversation.

We left after dark and on the way home, Dung reminded me to bring Cậu Năm some Holy Water that she had collected from her trip to Lourdes. I quietly kissed her hands, thanking God for our lives together.

Monday, January 5, 2009

One night my sister Huyền visited Cậu Năm while he was having massively violent coughing fits, so she decided to stay overnight to monitor his breathing. Since it was worse the next morning, she rushed him to the Emergency Room at Memorial Hospital.

A few days before, on the first of the New Year, Cậu Năm had found out that he had Stage Four lung cancer and he was depressed. He barely ate and his coughing had gotten much worse. My brothers, sisters and I took turns visiting him on a daily basis, and that really cheered him up. As days went by, he missed his children more and more and wanted desperately to see them.

Anh Quốc had gone back to Missouri to take care of personal matters, so Cậu Năm was lonelier than ever. I collected email addresses from our immediate relatives and made a point to send out regular emails to update our cousins and their families on Cậu Năm's condition. Huy Hoàng joined my efforts and kept everyone informed. Even with two very small children, Tí continued to come to his house everyday to deliver communion and pray with him. Huyền too came by regularly to make him feel respected and cherished.

Ever since coming to Houston, Cậu Năm had been close to Huyền. Her kindhearted nature and sharp personality reminded him of his own daughters. And just as she had always wanted, Huyền had become an Optometrist with two of her own successful clinics. One of her clinics was near Cậu Năm's residence, and this allowed him to visit and bring food. They got along splendidly and her office employees also loved to see him.

Whenever he had visited her clinic, he brought plenty of food for everyone. There were Vietnamese foods of *chả giò, gỏi gà, cháo gà, rau càng cua trộn sà lách, nem nướng, cá kho, thịt kho, bánh bao …* which are lunch dishes of chicken, rice, soup, salad, barbecued pork, fried fish … and there were pizzas as well. They sat, ate and had fun together. These relatively frequent visits meant much to my sister Huyền. Cậu Năm was lonely and treated her like one of his own; and she loved him for it.

When Cậu Năm got cancer, Huyền was very sad, but she tried her best to cheer him up. She took great care of him and treated him like her own father.

At the emergency room, Huyền checked Cậu Năm in and waited with him until they moved him into an ER room. The nurses and doctors stuck him with probes, hooked him up to instruments and injected him with drugs for the pain. Huyền left for work and we alternated coming in to watch over him.

Coincidentally, on the same morning, Huy Hoàng checked my Dad into the same hospital. In the past several years, my Dad had developed a heart condition, where one of his heart valves did not close or open properly. As a result, he tired easily and experienced severe headaches. A recent flu had left my Dad dehydrated to the point that he could no longer ingest food or liquids. Huy Hoàng took him to see a Vietnamese doctor, and the doctor immediately checked my Dad into the hospital.

Here they were: Two of the three heads of the family who had risked their lives on the high seas to deliver us to the land of freedom now in the same hospital. They had survived years of war in Vietnam, months in wretched refugee camps, and endured and humbled themselves to feed their families in the new land. Now they were again fighting for their lives.

Wednesday, January 8, 2009

Cậu Năm's condition was deteriorating quickly, while my Dad's health improved considerably after several days of saline intravenous injections. I had established a blog on the Internet and kept our relatives informed of what was going on. Anh Quốc had hurried back to be with his dad, and Cậu Năm was ecstatic to see his son again.

Shortly thereafter my Dad was well enough to be discharged and go home, but Cậu Năm's condition was getting worse. Here is an entry from Huy Hoàng:

> *"Cậu Năm has had a build up of fluids in his chest cavity that has exerted pressure on his lungs making it more difficult for him to breathe. The doctor wanted to perform a procedure that would consist of an injection of a highly caustic solution in through his chest tube, which would irritate his lungs and pleural cavity causing them to contract and to expel the excess fluids allowing him to breathe easier.*
>
> *"My Dad was discharged and walked over to Cậu Năm's room just before the doctors injected the solution into Cậu Năm's chest tube. My Dad sat down nervously and waited while I stayed for the procedure. Although Cậu Nam was given morphine before the procedure, the pain (burning) of the solution and the added pressure in his body was more than he could*

bear. He grabbed my hand and said 'Con, Cậu Năm chết!' Son, I am dying! I told him that I was going to hold onto him and not let that happen.

"I told the doctors that he could feel the burning from the solution and he was in tremendous pain. The doctors gave him more morphine and they were able to complete the procedure.

"My Dad was visibly shaken by witnessing this procedure, so I left to take my Dad back home to be with my Mom. When my Dad got home from the hospital, he told my Mom about the procedure he witnessed on Cậu Năm and that got her scared and anxious. She wants to visit Cậu Năm but is very fearful of seeing her dear brother in such a weakened condition.

"I had to stay overnight with my Mom because she has been very worried about both my Dad and Cậu Năm. She hadn't been eating. She had been pacing around the house anxiously, and her blood pressure had gotten very high. She had been nauseous and dizzy. I managed to coerce my Mom into eating last night and sat and listened to her stories until she was tired and she was ready to go to bed. I flopped down in my old bedroom and the next thing I knew, I was awakened by the sounds of my Mom fluttering around the house doing her morning chores. I got up and asked her if she was able to sleep through the night and she indicated that she had. She seemed to be doing better, so I went home."

Wednesday, January 14, 2009

Things got progressively worse for Cậu Năm. Anh Quốc sent emails and posted on our blog urgent requests for his family to come and visit Cậu Năm for the last time. And for me, it was difficult to concentrate at work. While thinking about Cậu Năm, my Mom and Dad and Dì Bảy all day, the issues of work seemed so unimportant.

Modern medicine of the most advanced country on earth and the minds of the greatest oncologists had failed Cậu Năm. They had given up on him and were moving him to the hospice, where there would be no more treatments, just oxygen and perhaps occasional pain killers. They taped a purple band around his right wrist that said DNR for *Do Not Resuscitate* or *Revive*. Once his lungs failed, they would let him go.

The email about moving Cậu Năm to the hospice blipped up upon my computer screen, and I was grateful to Anh Quốc for sending it out. I grabbed a couple of small empty boxes for moving and rushed to Memorial Hospital. I arrived at noon and saw Cậu Năm was resting. In the room were Anh Quốc, Chị Dạ Thu, my sister Hà, Dì Bảy's son named Sơn who is a doctor, Cô Lisa and two of her sons.

Anh Quốc cracked a tired smile welcoming me into the crowded room. He had been up all night with his father and was exhausted. His earlier email described how poor Cậu Năm had slept the last several nights. He had frequent nightmares and reacted violently to them. Anh Quốc was in no better shape, as he had spent every night lately at his dad's bedside. For only a couple of hours of sleep a night, Anh Quốc slept on a two by five cot under a cold window, and the past ten nights had taken a toll on his skinny body. He was unshaven and unkempt and his bloodshot eyes spoke of the pain he was in, and I wondered how this little man could still be so strong and have such a huge capacity for love.

And then, just as though someone reached out and turned off the switch to his air supply, Cậu Năm sat up and jerked his arms as if fighting some unseen enemy. His eyes opened wide, focusing elsewhere and nowhere. His expression was that of pure fear and horror. He tried to breathe and there was no air. He opened his mouth to yell but there was no sound. And he tried to grab but there was nothing to grab onto. He must have seen Death, but did not yet want to go.

Anh Quốc rushed to his side and tried to calm him down, but in his frenzy Cậu Năm was too powerful. Amid her tears, Chị Dạ Thu held his right arm down and kept saying, *"Ba, ráng thở đi Ba."* Dad, please keep breathing.

Hà held the oxygen mask on Cậu Năm's face and said, *"Cậu Năm không thở, Má con sẽ rày."* If you don't breathe, my Mom will be upset.

All the while, Cô Lisa stood next to the bed beside Anh Quốc, crying hysterically. Her two sons were standing there sobbing as well. Sơn rushed out of the room and asked the nurse for pain killers. The short little nurse rushed around and came back with a giant syringe full of God-knows-what. Sơn fought to hold Cậu Năm down so the nurse could administer the drug. I left the room to say a prayer for Cậu Năm and to call Dung.

I told Dung that Cậu Năm had seen Death and that he might not have much time left, and I could feel her heart tightening. Dung was choked up, "Are you okay?"

Only then did I realize that I too was crying. I didn't know if they were tears of fear or sadness, but I knew that I needed her more than ever. I told Dung that I love her.

I went back in the room and everything was quiet. The drug Sơn (the Doctor) ordered took effect immediately and Cậu Năm was out cold. His chest rose and fell laboriously. Anh Quốc, still shaken, quickly wiped his moist eyes and told me it had been much worse last night. I was afraid that he would burst out crying at any moment. Cô Lisa sat sniffling quietly in the corner. The woman seemed so small, lost and lonely. There was no way I could comfort her, just give her space and respect her pain, I told myself. The ever-present smile on Chi Dạ Thu's face was gone, as she stood silently by Cậu Năm, patting away the sweat on his forehead while tears rolled down her cheeks.

The Ambulance Transport arrived at exactly 1 PM and two big all-American men loaded the comatose man onto the gurney with ease. Anh Quốc automatically went into organizer-extraordinaire mode and gave instructions to everyone about where to go and what to do. I left to go pick up my parents and Dì Bảy who was staying with them at their house, and Anh Quốc left with Cậu Năm in the ambulance.

Hà had called ahead so my parents and Dì Bảy were ready by the time I pulled into the driveway. Dì Bảy had arrived in Houston from Cincinnati the night before and went straight to the hospital room to see Cậu Năm who was so happy to see my Mom and Dì Bảy that he fought the drugs to stay awake and talk to them. He held Dì Bảy's hand in one hand and my Mom's hand in the other. He smiled broadly, choked back tears and told them how much he loved them and that made both of them cry.

"Dì Bảy xuống được làm tôi mừng lắm. Tôi cứ sợ là sẽ chết trước khi gặp lại Dì," said Cậu Năm. I am so glad that you have made it down here to see me. I was afraid that I would die before I had a chance to see you again.

He smiled a painful smile as he struggled to form his sentences. *"Anh Năm ráng ăn uống để lấy sức. Tôi và mấy cháu sẽ cố lo lắng cho Anh,"* said Dì Bảy. Please try and eat for your strength. All of us will take care of you.

Then Dì Bảy wept, *"Mấy đứa con của Anh xấp về tới nơi rồi, nên ráng lên Anh ơi."* Your children are on their way here, please try to hold on longer.

He asked Dì Bảy about Dượng Bảy and her children, and then he told Dì Bảy and my Mom that he was about to die. *"Anh có chết, hai em nhớ cầu nguyện cho Anh"* When I die, please remember to pray for me.

My Mom could not control herself any longer, wept loudly and bowed down to kiss his hand. *"Anh Năm đừng bỏ tụi em,"* begged my Mom. Please don't leave us.

Cậu Năm looked at her lovingly and said, *"Cho Anh cám ơn mấy đứa con em. Tụi nó đã hy sinh và lo lắng cho Anh rất nhiều, Anh sẽ cầu xin Chúa ban ơn lành cho gia đình tụi em."* Please thank your children for me. They have taken care of me very well, and I will ask God to bless your family.

As Cậu Năm drifted back into sleep, Dì Bảy held my Mom's hand and cried, *"Anh Năm ốm quá vậy Chị. Cũng may là tôi đến đây kịp lúc."* He is so sick; I am so glad that I got here in time.

The two sisters held each other, weeping. They left the hospital shortly after that, and it was the last time they talked to their dear brother.

As I pulled up the driveway, my Dad was waiting for me in the garage. Without saying Hello, he asked, "How's Cậu Năm?" His concern for his best friend and the pain on his face made me tear up again. I told him that they had taken him away in an ambulance, and my Dad listened attentively and silently turned away to wipe his tears. It was difficult to see him weeping.

In the car, I related to my Mom and Dì Bảy what had transpired earlier in the day. My Mom sobbed non stop and Dì Bảy too was sniffling. Dì Bảy is such a good sister to my Mom. Unlike my Mom who is always strict and reserved, Dì Bảy is sweet and gentle. Of all the years that I have known her and her family, I have never heard her raise her voice while talking to her children. Her presence was so comforting to everyone around her.

At the new hospital, I parked in the wrong parking lot, and we had to walk quite a way to the hospice. It was a beautiful but cold day in Houston. I walked briskly carrying Cậu Năm's and Anh Quốc's baggage and belongings from the old hospital. Behind me, the two sisters walked hand-in-hand, huddling together against the cold wind that was blowing between the buildings. Farther behind was my Dad pacing slowly, but as fast as his heart would let him. I said a simple prayer and thanked God for family.

When we arrived at Cậu Năm's hospice room and my Mom saw him laying there on the bed, helplessly unconscious, she completely succumbed to her heart. She wept intensely and held on to Anh Quốc as though she was about to faint. Anh Quốc had to take my Mom away to the visitor's room and sat her down on the sofa to calm her down. Meanwhile, Dì Bảy, her eyes already reddened, were filled up again with tears that spilled down her face. She held onto my Mom, comforting her and at the same time getting comforted.

After I helped the nurse change the soiled linen below Cậu Năm, I went out to the visitor's lounge to fetch my Mom, who at this time could not even walk by herself. The grief in seeing Cậu Năm in such condition was too overwhelming.

In the hospice room, Cậu Năm was still unconscious and struggling for every breath. He looked old and dried-up. My Mom and Dì Bảy sat on the sofa crying their hearts out. My Dad sat near the windows, his lips moving slightly as he prayed. Chị Dạ Thu, Chị Dạ Thảo the youngest girl in Cậu Năm's family, Anh Quốc, Dr. Sơn and I hovered around not knowing what to do, but just being there.

Tí came in the room and wanted to start a prayer vigil. Thank God for Tí. As they started the rosary, I sneaked out to go pick up Mợ Năm, who was arriving at Hobby Airport. Chị Dạ Thảo wanted to go with me, but I could not take her away from her Dad. And besides, I needed to be alone.

In the car, I called Anh Hùng and found out that he had just arrived at the hospice. I called Chị Lêvi and she said she still had the flu and could not visit Cậu Năm. I then called Anh Hưng to let him know and he said that he would get there as soon as he could leave work. I didn't know why I called them, but perhaps I wanted to make sure that the bonds between us siblings were still as strong as what I had witnessed between Mom, Dì Bảy and Cậu Năm.

At the airport, I watched a short, tiny woman in her early seventies walk slowly out of the gate and when she saw me her eyes lit up. Even though we had not seen each other for over thirty years, something inside me told me this was Mợ Năm.

Mợ Năm smiled softly and said, *"Con Ông Chính, phải không?"* Mr. Chinh's son, right?

And she proceeded to tell me how much I look like my Dad. She walked slowly and held onto my hand as we went to pick up her luggage.

On the way to the hospice, Mợ Năm was nervous and anxious, yet she chatted incessantly for an hour while we were in traffic. She talked about God, religion and her recurring dreams; then she talked about her family and her church. She became more agitated when we arrived at the hospice. She quieted down while we walked down the hall and finally asked me, *"Cậu Năm sao con?"* How's Cậu Năm?

I told her Cậu Năm was in bad shape and that I was certain that he and her children would be so happy to see her. She was not pleased with my reply, but resigned. Upon entering the room, Mợ Năm was quickly overwhelmed by her children, Chị Dạ Thảo, Chị Dạ Thu and Anh Quốc; yet she must have felt awkward being with Cô Lisa in the same room. Noticing that my parents and Dì Bảy had gone home, I quickly and gladly left to go to the Houston International Airport to pick up two of Cậu Năm's sons, Anh Kiệt and Anh Bé.

On the way, I picked up Dung. She had been by my side every day for the past two weeks comforting Cậu Năm, and Cậu Năm said that he would bless both of us once he got to Heaven. Dung just nodded and smiled, showing her dimples. God, I love her.

We stopped by a Vietnamese restaurant on the way so I could gulp down some *"cháo lòng"* (rice soup). I hadn't realized that I had not eaten anything all day. We ate quickly and made it to the airport in time to pick up Anh Kiệt and Anh Bé.

They were tired from traveling, but just like Mợ Năm, Anh Kiệt chatted away, hiding his anxiousness, while Anh Bé quietly wept. Every time Anh Bé tried to strike up a conversation, he could only muster a few words before choking up. Anh Bé reminisced about growing up in Vietnam with Cậu Năm and his taxiing him around on his Vespa scooter after work. Anh Bé had just come back from Vietnam and still carried with him its sights, sounds and ambiance in his heart, I guessed.

We ran into my sister Lêvi and her husband Anh Sơn in the hospice's parking lot. I knew Chị Lêvi still felt the effects of a cold, but I was overjoyed to see my older sister who had left a warm bed so she could pay her respects to Cậu Năm while he was still alive.

When we entered the hospice room, Cậu Năm was unconscious, but a crowd had gathered around him. Mợ Năm, Dạ Thu, Dạ Thảo, Anh Quốc, Cậu Năm's other son Anh Vũ, and now Anh Kiệt and Anh Bé. Dì Bảy's son Dr. Sơn, my brother Huy-Hoàng, Hà, Tí, Huyền, Anh Hưng and Anh Hùng were there.

Anh Kiệt took lots of pictures of everyone. He said that they had not had a grand reunion for such a long time and, needing a family picture, proceeded to click away. Anh Bé had just flown back to the US from Vietnam after receiving the pleading posting on the blog from Anh Quốc. Seeing Cậu Năm on the verge of death broke his heart.

In a Vietnamese family it was traditional for the oldest son to look after his aging parents. If one of the parents died, the oldest son was responsible for gathering the family and attending to the funeral arrangements. But since the fallout between Cậu Năm and Mợ Năm, the relationship between Cậu Năm and his oldest son Anh Dzuy had been seriously strained. After his parents' separation, Anh Dzuy had moved to California and had had very little contact with Cậu Năm.

The next oldest son was Anh Tân, but Anh Tân was a priest now. He belonged to God and Cậu Năm did not wish to burden Father Tân with his trouble; so more than a year before Cậu Năm became critically ill, he called Anh Bé, the next son in line.

The phone call shocked Anh Bé because he was the last person he thought the old man would choose to look after his affairs. Anh Bé had always been a troubled child and his mischievous behavior had caused Cậu Năm and Mợ Năm a lot of worry.

Anh Bé had constantly picked fights at school and refused to study hard like the rest of Cậu Năm's children. And things got so bad that Cậu Năm eventually had to send Anh Bé to live with Ông Ngoại for a long time.

However, Anh Bé's fearless attitude and irreverence for authority reminded Cậu Năm so much of himself in the younger days. He truly loved Anh Bé, but had never been able to express how deeply he loved his child. Cậu Năm always knew in his heart that Anh Bé loved him too and would do anything for him.

"Nếu Ba có chết thì Ba muốn con là người đứng ra lo lắng công việc chôn cất cho Ba," Cậu Năm said over the phone. If I die, I would like you to take care of the funeral arrangements.

"Ủa, Ba bị gì vậy?" What, are you okay? Anh Bé was shocked and he asked again, *"Ba có sao không?"* Is everything okay with you?

"Ba không bị gì cả, mà chỉ muốn con lo lắng cho Ba thôi. Tao đâu có chết đâu mà sợ," said Cậu Năm. I am well. I just want you to take care of me if anything happens. I am not dying, so don't be afraid.

"Ba đừng có lo. Con sẽ lo cho Ba," Anh Bé responded convincingly to Cậu Năm's request. Don't worry, Dad. I will take care of you.

Cậu Năm wanted to be cremated and have his ashes brought back to Nha Trang to be kept at Nhà Thờ Chợ Mới (Cho Moi Church) where he used to attend mass every Sunday. He offered his son money that he had saved for his funeral, but Anh Bé refused to take it from his father. Instead Anh Bé paid cash in advance for the total amount of the crematory services and all of the funeral arrangements. He also promised Cậu Năm that he would bring the ashes back home, as Cậu Năm had wished.

Seeing how frail Cậu Năm looked lying on the hospice bed distressed Anh Bé. He held onto Cậu Năm's hand and wept openly. It was like witnessing the return of a prodigal son making good on a promise. I was grateful that God had given both Cậu Năm and his son Anh Bé the chance to do right for each other.

At 10 o'clock in the evening, Cậu Năm's oldest son Anh Dzuy and his wife Chị Chi arrived at the hospice. They had just flown in from California and my oldest brother Hùng had picked them up at the airport. We gathered around Cậu Năm and tried to wake him. My sister Huyền talked to him in an effort to elicit some response, and he moved ever so slightly, trying hard to wake up. I whispered into Cậu Năm's ear that Anh Dzuy was here and wanted to talk to him, but all we could get out of Cậu Năm was a slight squeezing of our hands and an attempt to open his eyes. Anh Dzuy, Anh Bé and all of Cậu Năm's children talked to him, as our family (members of Dì Sáu's family and Sơn) moved to the Quiet Room nearby to give Cậu Mợ Năm and their children some privacy.

Seven of his ten children were by his side that night. Anh Tân (Father Tân) was on a mission in Vietnam and was on his way back; Cậu Năm's other daughter Chị Lan Anh and his other son Anh Hào were in transit. From those that were by Cậu Năm's side, we heard their joyous laughter and saw their tears of sadness and a rare family togetherness. I wished that Cậu Năm was coherent enough to see this. Perhaps he would rebound, perhaps he would laugh and cry, and perhaps he would finally go in peace.

That night, again Anh Quốc stayed with Cậu Năm in the hospice room overnight, and we all gradually departed. Anh Kiệt and Anh Bé stayed at our home, and we were up to 1 o'clock in the morning catching up. It had been quite a long time since we were last together, and I was glad to see them again.

The following day, the rest of Cậu Năm's children came to see him. Anh Hào and his wife Quỳnh arrived early in the morning, and soon Chị Lan Anh appeared with a friend of hers. After a long trip all the way from Vietnam, even Father Tân showed up.

Several of Dì Bảy's children flew down to Houston to say good-bye to Cậu Năm and to be with their mom. Thu, Dì Bảy's oldest daughter cried her heart out upon seeing Cậu Năm's condition. Thu called her other siblings to let them know, and her little sisters Trâm and Susie and Dì Bảy's oldest son Trung flew down the following day.

Cậu Năm's entire family was now assembled to say good-bye. At this time, Cậu Năm was so weak and heavily sedated that all he could do were to blink his eyes and squeeze their hands. But he knew they were there and this must have brought him much joy on his last day.

Epilogue

Cậu Năm died at 1:11 AM on Sunday, January 18, 2009.

His son, Father Tân, said the memorial mass at my parents' house. My parents and Dì Bảy offered their eulogies in front of the extended family and everyone wept openly.

On Monday, we had the funeral mass for Cậu Năm at St. Francis DeSalle. Father Tân and Father Huy said the Mass, and Anh Quốc delivered a touching eulogy. Afterward, most of the people flew or drove back home. Anh Quốc stayed in Houston with Cô Lisa.

...

On Thursday, January 22, at 10:30 AM when Anh Quốc stepped up to push the red button on the incinerator for the cremation of Cậu Năm's body, the finality of death hit my Mom really hard. She wept sorrowfully and her body shook as she fought to regain her composure. She acted as if she could not breathe, as though her heart was about to stop, as if she could feel the flames consuming Cậu Năm's body.

Her face contorted with pain and her tears poured out in torrents. She repeatedly murmured, *"Lạy Chúa tôi, lạy Chúa tôi."* Oh My God, oh My God.

She seemed fragile, vulnerable and helpless. I put my arms around my Mom to prevent her from falling, and later wondered who I was trying to support. Was she the one who needed someone to hold onto or was it me?

During the hospitalization and passing of Cậu Năm, I have seen more tears from my Mom than I have witnessed throughout my whole life. I saw a different kind of crying this morning. Thirty-four years in a strange land surrounded by strange customs and language have aged my mother into a different kind of person. A once successful entrepreneur was now an old woman, lost and confused about how to behave in this natural yet odd situation in a new culture.

The loss of familiarity and the comfort of old customs compounded by the loss of her beloved brother were too much for her. She saw her world collapsing all around her. Her expectations and assumptions were no longer valid. She looked around and saw only a handful of her kinfolk at the final ceremony. She felt the loneliness of a brother that was barely older than she. She sensed the heat of a mechanical machine called the incinerator, and knew that Cậu Năm would have no grave to visit. And she cried.

She missed her older sisters in Vietnam and thought about how they would react to the news of the passing of Cậu Năm. Would they keep the fond memories of their only brother? Would they appreciate his life and works here in the States? And would they be aware of the sacrifice that he had made for his children in this land? And she cried.

She thought about Cậu Năm's children and how often they would remember their father. Would they honor the Vietnamese tradition of saying a prayer for him every year on the day of his death? Or would they be too busy with their American life to even give him a passing thought? And would the grandchildren know anything about him? And she cried.

Perhaps she cried for Cậu Năm and perhaps she cried for herself. Those tears could have been for her old days in Vietnam, for growing up in the land of familiarity full of friends and relatives, for her father's native language and customs, and perhaps for a glorious past. Only my Mom knew for certain, but somehow I felt in her the self-pity of a lonesome woman.

As the temperature readings of the incinerator climbed to 1,800 degrees, my Mom sat dumbfounded, staring blankly into the vacant space in front of her. Tears streamed down her face. She seemed to have aged ten years within the last ten days. Her eyes sunk deeply into her colorless face and the glasses on her face could hardly hide the bags under her eyes. Her hair was unkempt and grayed. Her hands were cold and unsteady. She was among family, yet so alone. I stood by her side and my heart cried along with her.

Finally, Mom stood up with great effort and thanked each visitor as they came up to her and offered condolences. She regained her poise and refined manner. Then Anh Quốc did the perfect thing. He gave her the framed picture of Cậu Năm. Mom took it and held onto it, and for a brief moment, I saw the tremendous comfort in her eyes. She still had her beloved brother.

...

After the cremation service, I walked my parents to their car. My Mom was still stricken with grief. My Dad held the door open for her, turned to me and waved good-bye, *"Cám ơn nhe Vui. Thôi con về đi làm đi."* Thank you for being here, Vui. Go ahead and go back to work. His shoulder sank low and his eyes were still red, but he pushed for normalcy. My Dad, my hero of war and peace, seemed so meek and vulnerable.

As I made the right turn onto Gessner Street and their car disappeared from the rear view mirror, I suddenly bursted out in tears. Their generation is dying off. Would their children and grandchildren remember them and their sacrifice?

...

Anh Bé took Cậu Năm's ashes back to Vietnam, where Dì Hai, Dì Ba and Dì Bốn said good-bye to their younger brother. On February 9, they placed the ashes on the mausoleum wall of Nhà Thờ Chợ Mới, as instructed by Cậu Năm.

...

For the longest time I was oblivious about the Vietnam War, even while my Dad was risking his life every day defending the country. We lived in Saigon in relative peace, where many folks just did not pay any attention to the harsh reality of war. Furthermore, I was in the seminary and was taught to avoid conflict and to focus on peace, faith, hope and love. The romantic notion of resolving issues through discussion and peaceful resolution was all that I knew. Even after the war when we were living in the US, I had a truly hard time trying to comprehend what had actually happened back in the old country and what were the reasons for my Dad's intense hatred toward the communists.

In writing this book, I kept asking myself why I was writing it and for whom. In my soul searching, I kept coming back to the image of my Mom walking hand-in-hand with Dì Bảy, my Dad lagging behind, on the way to visit Cậu Năm at the hospice. I realized that this forgotten generation that will soon pass away had so much to tell.

...

The Vietnam War yielded no winner. And the biggest losers and yet the ultimate winners are this forgotten generation of Vietnamese expatriates *Việt-Kiều*.

My Dad and his generation risked their lives every day defending South Vietnam against the communists, and then at the end of the War, they gave up everything they had ever owned, even their friends and families and the country they grew up in, to deliver their children to the land of freedom. Once in the US, they humbled themselves performing whatever jobs they can find and against all odds kept their children in schools and gave them the opportunities to compete in this land.

While the Communist Vietnamese had rewritten history to their favor, the courageous and heroic accounts of the people of the South were blatantly disregarded. And while Americans were quick to put the memory of the Vietnam War behind them, the whole generation of South Vietnamese like my parents was completely forgotten. Yet it was because of them that my generation, their children grown up in America, would have the opportunities to better our lives.

The passing of Cậu Năm brought our families back together to say good bye to one of the three heads of households that had delivered us to this land. I wanted to memorialize the sacrifices of their generation and I wanted my children and grandchildren to remember them as well.

The forgotten generation has so much to tell, and I want to tell some small part of their sacrifice. To me, the forgotten generation are the winners.

Vui Le

Acknowledgments

The Author wishes to thank the following people:

My wife Young Le for her dedication, encouragement and support
of my efforts;
My Dad, the unsung hero;
My family for encouraging me and for keeping me straight on all
the facts.

Many thanks also go to the members of the Cậu Năm and Dì Bảy
families.

To Cậu Năm:

The Lord bless you and keep you
The Lord let His Face shine upon you
and be gracious to you
The Lord look kindly upon you and give you peace.

Nm 6:24-26